CW00664307

THE
DEFINITIVE
GUIDE TO TOK
IN THE IB

THE DEFINITIVE GUIDE TO TOK IN THE IB

HOW TO ACE THE THEORY OF KNOWLEDGE
ESSAY AND EXHIBITION

ANDREW M. CROSS

IB DP BOOKS

This book is printed on acid-free paper.

Copyright © 2022 Andrew M. Cross. All rights reserved.

No part of this book may be used or reproduced in any manner whatsoever without written permission, except in the case of brief quotations embodied in critical articles or reviews.

Published 2022 IB DP Publishing

ISBN 978-1-7391851-0-7, paperback

Dedicated to all TOK teachers.

TABLE OF CONTENTS

INTRODUCTION   1
CHAPTER 1: THE BASICS   3
   TOK IN A NUTSHELL   4
CHAPTER 2: THE TOK ESSAY   7
   ASSESSMENT   8
   PRESCRIBED TITLES   13
   KNOWLEDGE QUESTIONS   20
   STRUCTURING THE ESSAY   27
   REAL - LIFE EXAMPLES   32
   INTRODUCTION   37
   ARGUMENTS   42
   CONCLUSION   47
CHAPTER 3: THE TOK EXHIBITION   49
   ASSESSMENT   50
   WHERE TO START   53
   CHOOSING THE IA PROMPT   56
   HOW TO CHOOSE THE OBJECTS   58
   WRITING THE COMMENTARIES   63
   WRITING THE INTRODUCTION   65
CHAPTER 4: TEN GRADE-A TOK ESSAYS   71
   EXAMPLE 1   73
   EXAMPLE 2   79
   EXAMPLE 3   85
   EXAMPLE 4   91
   EXAMPLE 5   99
   EXAMPLE 6   103
   EXAMPLE 7   109
   EXAMPLE 8   117
   EXAMPLE 9   123
   EXAMPLE 10   131

INTRODUCTION

This book is prepared to help you understand the TOK course better, have a deeper insight into the assessments and put theoretical knowledge in practice. The first short chapter "TOK in a Nutshell" briefly explains the course.

The second chapter "TOK Essay" explains TOK assessments in general and how to write a TOK essay and get a good mark. Try to read every sentence in every page and feel free to use the methods, however, as it is explained in the chapter, do not copy the sample texts, as it is considered a violation and your essay may be penalized due to the fact that IB has no tolerance for plagiarism.

The third and the fourth chapters are dedicated to the TOK exhibition.

The third chapter explains the exhibition as TOK IA, and guides you to create a great exhibition with a great mark. Again, feel free to use the examples and suggestions, however, do not copy the sample texts, because of the same reason that I explained above.

The fourth chapter is 10 examples of excellent TOK essay. All of these essays have scored a grade A and are considered some of the best examples of student work.

Enjoy reading and good luck!

CHAPTER 1: THE BASICS

TOK IN A NUTSHELL

This is a brief introduction to the IBDP TOK course.

"What is the title of this chapter?"

If I asked you this question, you would answer "TOK in a Nutshell. " That is right, however, how do you know that? You may answer that you have read it at the top of the page. This is TOK, as simple as this.

When you "claim" to have "knowledge", you should also be able to justify your "knowledge claim" and provide some "evidence" for it.

Another important aspect is that TOK is NOT philosophy. "Theory of Knowledge" is a branch of philosophy, also known as "epistemology".

You can see many similarities between the two, however the purpose of the TOK course is not to discuss philosophy or to get philosophical about everything. On the contrary, the TOK course is designed to train you to have a critical look on whatever you face throughout your life, and at the same time, to consider other points of view. This is the reason that TOK is one of the "core "elements of IBDP, alongside EE and CAS.

Throughout the course, the "core theme", two "optional themes "out of five, five "areas of knowledge "and assessments (TOK Exhibition and Essay) should be taught and explained to you by your TOK teacher, in a total of minimum 100 teaching hours.

The core theme is called Knowledge and The Knower. Five optional themes are Knowledge and Technology, Knowledge and Language, Knowledge and Politics, Knowledge and Religion and Knowledge and Indigenous Societies. The Areas of Knowledge are History, The Human Sciences, The Natural Sciences, The Arts and Mathematics.

All these themes and AOKs (areas of knowledge) will be explored within the four elements of "knowledge framework" which are scope, perspectives, methods and tools and ethics.

Knowledge is also believed to have deep connections with 12 concepts:

evidence, certainty, truth, interpretation, power, justification, explanation, objectivity, perspective, culture, values and responsibility.

And finally, Knowledge Questions. KQs are open-ended, contestable, thought-provoking questions that need to be explored (not answered per se).

You can find more information and explanations in TOK coursebooks.

CHAPTER 2: THE TOK ESSAY

ASSESSMENT

At the end of the day, for most students, it's not about knowledge, self-development or becoming a successful visionary individual in society. It's all about the '"exams" and the "marks". So, let's talk about them.

TOK essay is the external assessment component, with 2/3 (67%) weighting. The essay is also marked out of 10 marks. What do all these means?

It is not that complicated. You write an essay on a prescribed title! Your essay will be marked out of 10 by IB examiners (not your TOK teacher). Then the mark given to your essay will be multiplied by 2 and will be added to your exhibition mark. In result, the student, you, receives a total mark, for TOK, out of 30. Then there are grade boundaries (A - E).

Overall/30	E	D	C	B	A
	0-3	4-9	10-15	16-21	22-30

The above chart is based on the latest grade boundaries published by IB. The boundaries may have little alterations from year to year, but this is what you can count on to have an insight.

Let's have some LEs (Real-life examples):

Imagine a student receives 6/10 for their essay and 8/10 for the exhibition. The total mark will be 20/30 (6x2+8). Based on the chart above, this student receives B for their TOK.

You may receive a 7/10 for your exhibition. In this case, at least you need an 8/10 for your essay to have an A in total.

These boundaries, alongside other marks and grades, later will be used to determine the student's final point (out of 45).

Before getting into how to write a TOK essay, understanding the titles and the development process, there are some technical guidelines that you should be aware of.

TOK Essay specification:

- ✓ The TOK essay must be written in standard font size 12 and double spaced.

- ✓ The maximum length of the essay is 1,600 words, including the main part and any quotations. (Examiners stop reading the essay after 1,600 words).

- ✓ Acknowledgments, references, maps, charts, diagrams etc. and the bibliography are not included in the word count.

- ✓ Extended notes, extensive footnotes or appendices are not appropriate and may not be read.

- ✓ Students must indicate the number of words when the essay is uploaded.

As you can see, it is crucial for the student to keep the essay less than 1,600 words, even if just by 1 word, to be on the safe side.

The following chart shows the criteria based on which TOK essay is assessed:

| Does the student provide a clear, coherent and critical exploration of the essay title? |

The assessment instrument provided describes five levels of performance in response to this driving question. These levels are to be seen as holistic descriptors rather than as a checklist of characteristics.

Does the student provide a clear, coherent and critical exploration of the essay title?					
Excellent 9-10	Good 7-8	Satisfactory 5-6	Basic 3-4	Rudimentary 1-2	0
The discussion has a sustained focus on the title and is linked effectively to areas of knowledge. Arguments are clear, coherent and effectively supported by specific examples. The implications of arguments are considered. There is clear awareness and evaluation of different points of view.	The discussion is focused on the title and is linked effectively to areas of knowledge. Arguments are clear, coherent and supported by examples. There is awareness and some evaluation of different points of view.	The discussion is focused on the title and is developed with some links to areas of knowledge. Arguments are offered and are supported by examples. There is some awareness of different points of view.	The discussion is connected to the title and makes superficial or limited links to areas of knowledge. The discussion is largely descriptive. Limited arguments are offered but they are unclear and are not supported by effective examples.	The discussion is weakly connected to the title. While there may be links to the areas of knowledge, any relevant points are descriptive or consist only of unsupported assertions.	The discussion does not reach the standard described by the other levels or is not a response to one of the prescribed titles for the correct examination session.
Possible characteristics					
Insightful Convincing Accomplished Lucid	Pertinent Relevant Analytical Organized	Acceptable Mainstream Adequate Competent	Underdeveloped Basic Superficial Limited	Ineffective Descriptive Incoherent Formless	

11

In simple terms, an Excellent TOK essay must be focused on the title and does not get distracted from the main discussion. Arguments must be clearly explored within the Areas of Knowledge (although recently we see some exceptions, like title #2 for N21). Your arguments (and counterarguments) must be developed in a coherent way, supported by real-life examples. The student must also consider the implications of their arguments, which means you should also consider others' interpretations of your arguments. And lastly, your text must show that you are fully aware of other points of views, and you are not trying to project your biased view on the topic.

In the following chapters, we will discuss how to fully understand and choose the title, how to develop your arguments and, in general, how to write an excellent TOK essay, through detailed explanations and examples.

PRESCRIBED TITLES

Prescribed titles, on which TOK essay must be written, are released by IB six months before the submission deadline. At least this is what's written in the guide. What you may want to know is that May students can expect their titles in September (of the previous year), and November students can receive them in March. Each year, IB releases two sets of prescribed titles, each containing 6 titles. Students should choose one title and write 1,600 words on it within two areas of knowledge. This condition was altered for the November '21 (and some older) session, and it seems IB is going to be more creative/flexible in the following years. The most important thing that you, as an IB student, need to know is how to choose the right title, which means the title that is best for you and you can write a TOK essay on it using your maximum potential.

But how'd you know which of the 6 titles is the best one for you? Well, we're going to find out in 3 easy steps:

1. Read all the titles and see if there's any keyword that attracts you or maybe sounds familiar (e.g. trust, progress, labels, statistics, combination or bias). Then sort the titles based on "attractiveness" and break down each into 3 simple sentences. For instance, "labels are a necessity in the organization of knowledge, but they also constrain our understanding." This can be broken down

into "labels are necessary," 'labels help categorizing knowledge," and 'labels limit our understanding'.

2. Leave your notes aside and come back to them after a couple of days. Read the simple versions (preferably with a friend) and see which ones make more sense. Move 3 more sensible titles to the top of the list. Then try to explain them to a person with absolutely no TOK knowledge, and carefully observe their facial reactions!

3. Find two relevant AOKs for each title and write them next to the top three. Now take a step back and see if your eye catches your favourite AOKs. Which title do they belong to? That's the title you're going to write your essay about.

If you still have doubts, or are too lazy to do these steps, or maybe do not trust yourself with this task, then definitely your TOK teacher is there to help you choose the best title. You can also do research and read titles explanations by internet resources to have a better understanding of them. To make it more practical, let's choose the best title from the released list for the May '22 session.

The following is the first page of the document, giving you instructions:

Theory of knowledge prescribed titles

- Your theory of knowledge essay must be written on one of the six essay titles (questions) provided overleaf. These essay titles take the form of knowledge questions that are focused on the areas of knowledge. You may choose any of the titles but are recommended to make your choice in consultation with your teacher.

- Your essay will be marked according to the assessment instrument published in the theory of knowledge guide.

- Examiners will be looking to see that you have provided a clear, coherent and critical exploration of your chosen title.

- Examiners will mark your essay against the title as set. It is very important that you respond to the title exactly as given and do not alter the title in any way. Please note that any quotations that appear in the titles are not necessarily authentic. They will present a real point of view but may not be direct quotations.

- Your theory of knowledge essay must be submitted to your teacher for authentication. Any external sources used must be acknowledged and should be cited according to a recognized convention.

Your theory of knowledge essay should be written in standard size 12 font and be double spaced. It must be a maximum of 1600 words.

And these are the titles:

1. Can there be knowledge that is independent of culture? Discuss with reference to mathematics and one other area of knowledge.

2. To what extent do you agree with the claim that "there's a world of difference between truth and facts"(Maya Angelou)? Answer with reference to two areas of knowledge.

3. Is there solid justification for regarding knowledge in the natural sciences more highly than knowledge in another area of knowledge? Discuss with reference to the natural sciences and one other area of knowledge.

4. How do historians and human scientists give knowledge meaning
through the telling of stories? Discuss with reference to history and the human sciences.

5. How can we distinguish between good and bad interpretations? Discuss with reference to the arts and one other area of knowledge.

6. If we conclude that there is some knowledge we should not pursue on ethical grounds, how can we determine the boundaries of acceptable investigation within an area of knowledge? Discuss with reference to two areas of knowledge.

The first step is to find "attractive" words or phrases. If you are a Math-lover then you'll find title #1 very interesting, however you should be very careful as your bias may get the best of you. If you like quotes and challenges, most probably you'll find title #2 the most attractive. I guess all "real science" students would aim for title #3, as they can brag about how real science is more solid than other AOKs. I'm not sure if anyone, at your age, finds title #4 attractive, but story-telling may be someone's "things" and they can find this title interesting enough to choose. Title #5 is surely for people with high analytical skills, students who are always good and "compare and contrast". And finally, title #6 is for those who hold ethics in a very high regard, or the ones who are absolutely against it. Both can bring strong and interesting arguments, and counterarguments.

The next step is to break down the titles and simplify them.

1. Can there be knowledge that is independent of culture? Discuss with reference to mathematics and one other area of knowledge.

2. To what extent do you agree with the claim that "there's a world of difference between truth and facts"(Maya Angelou)? Answer with reference to two areas of knowledge.

3. Is there solid justification for regarding knowledge in the natural sciences more highly than knowledge in another area of knowledge? Discuss with reference to the natural sciences and one other area of knowledge.

4. How do historians and human scientists give knowledge meaning through the telling of stories? Discuss with reference to history and the human sciences.

5. How can we distinguish between good and bad interpretations? Discuss with reference to the arts and one other area of knowledge.

6. If we conclude that there is some knowledge we should not pursue on ethical grounds, how can we determine the boundaries of acceptable investigation within an area of knowledge? Discuss with reference to two areas of knowledge.

And the last step, after taking your mind off for a couple of days, is to fine relevant AOKs for each title.

Title #1 already has Mathematics, and any of the other four AOKs can be chosen to explore within. History seems like the first obvious choice for title #2, and The Human Sciences, especially the discipline of Law could be a good companion. The Natural Sciences and Mathematics are also gold mines of facts that can be used to develop counterarguments within

The Natural Sciences is already chosen for title #3, and if you intend to argue against the title, you will choose Mathematics, and to argue pro the title, The Natural Sciences is your second choice. Title #4 already has its two AOKs selected. The Arts is already chosen as one of the AOKs for title #5 and any of the other four AOKs are relevant and good choices. Lastly, title #6 is about ethics, and what AK is better than The Human Sciences to discuss ethics within? The Arts, The Natural sciences and History are good candidates for the second AOK.

Whether you use this method, follow your teacher's guidance or ask a random stranger to choose a number from one to six, it is crucial to break down and simplify the titles, and choose proper and relevant AOKs for your chosen title. Try to choose an AOK that you have enough knowledge about and may already have one of two RLEs related to the title in mind.

KNOWLEDGE QUESTIONS

Knowledge Questions (KQs) are the essence of TOK. KQs are thought- provoking open-ended questions to be explored within different Areas of Knowledge. Every TOK essay needs at least two knowledge questions, one for each area of knowledge, or one to argue the claim and one for the counterclaim. Please keep in mind that the student does not have to write the knowledge questions in their essay. You can use the KQs that you develop (in your notes), only as guiding questions to be answered/explored throughout your essay.

For sure, students face, explore, and probably develop many of these knowledge questions during the course. The difference between a not-KQ and a KQ can be seen through the following examples:

• "How can we measure the mass of an object?"(NOT a KQ)

• "How can we know the method that we use for measuring the mass of an object brings us the most accurate results?"(a KQ)

• "Can bias play a positive role in the advancement of knowledge?"(NOT a KQ)

• To what extent does bias play a positive role in the advancement of knowledge?"(a KQ)

By now, you can probably distinguish between "direct" questions and KQs. And you are possibly able to explore (answer) them. However, the question remains on how to form/develop a good knowledge question. Well, you can practice and achieve forming viable knowledge questions for your essays in the following three steps:

1. Write up to 10 direct questions about the title that you have chosen for your essay. Let's say you choose "statistics conceal as much as they reveal." Your direct questions might be "what do statistics conceal?" or "do statistics conceal more than they reveal?" etc.

2. Divide the questions into two groups, pro and against the title. If the answer to the question implies that statistics conceal information, then that question is pro the title and can be used for your claim and the other way around for the counterclaim.

3. And finally, add "the elements of ambiguity"("to what extent," "how can we," etc.) to your direct questions and ask them within an area of knowledge. Your possible knowledge questions might look like "to what extent do statistics

conceal information in the natural sciences?" or "how is it possible to know if statistics conceal vital information when presented as a part of a historical knowledge claim?" etc.

You can improve and develop these simple knowledge questions into more explorable ones worthy of your TOK essay. If you are not satisfied with this simplified method, you can continue reading and learn more, otherwise, do not spend more time on knowledge questions and simply jump to the next chapter.

The new TOK guide (first assessment 2022) recommends five optional themes, two of which must be selected and taught by the teacher throughout the course, in addition to, strongly linked to, and extended from the core theme (knowledge and the knower). These five themes are knowledge and technology, knowledge and language, knowledge and politics, knowledge and religion, and knowledge and indigenous societies. At the same time, four compulsory elements (scope, perspectives, methods and tools, and ethics) are required in every part of the syllabus.

The good news is that the TOK guide has also provided us with numerous well-structured knowledge questions that we can adjust/develop according to the essay's title. One of the most common optional themes is knowledge and language. The following chart, and connecting KQs, bring great knowledge questions within this theme, with links to the core theme under the four elements.

	Examples of knowledge questions
Scope	· Can all knowledge be expressed in words or symbols? · Is it possible to think or know without language? · Is being able to speak a language an example of "knowing how" to do something? · What role does language play in allowing knowledge to be shared with future generations? · Are there differences in how knowledge itself is conceived of, or presented, in different languages? · Is it the case that if we cannot express something, we don't know it? · To what extent does language allow us to make our private experiences public? · How does language allow humans to pool resources and share knowledge?
Perspectives	· Does the transmission of knowledge from one person or generation to another · depend on language?

	· What knowledge might be lost if the whole world shared one common language?
	· If a language dies, does knowledge die with it?
	· How do our values and assumptions influence the language in which we express our ideas?
	· Is ambiguity a shortcoming of language that must be eliminated, or can it also be seen as making a positive contribution to knowledge and knowing?
	· Do all people share some innate linguistic knowledge? If the categories that we use necessarily empower or marginalise, is it ever possible to produce knowledge that does not either reflect or challenge existing power structures?
Methods And Tools	· How are metaphors used in the construction of knowledge?
	· If language works according to sets of rules and conventions, how much scope do we have as individuals to break the rules or challenge these conventions?
	· In what ways do values affect our representations of the world, for example, in language, maps or visual images?
	· To what extent do the classification systems we use in the pursuit of knowledge affect the conclusions that we reach?
	· In what ways can language be used to influence, persuade or manipulate people's emotions?
	· To what extent do the names and labels that we use help or hinder the acquisition of knowledge?
Ethics	· Does ethical language differ in any significant way from other types of language?
	· How can we know if language is intended to deceive or manipulate us?
	· Do ethical statements simply convey our feelings/emotions rather than making claims?
	· If ethical terms and concepts cannot be easily defined, does this mean that they are meaningless?

	· Can we define words such as good and bad in terms of objective features of the world?
	· Do professional interpreters and translators have any special ethical obligations?

Making connections to the core theme

• If you speak more than one language, is what you know different in each language? (scope)

• Do people from different linguistic or cultural backgrounds live, in some sense, in different worlds? (perspectives)

• What are the implications if we do not produce knowledge in language that respects people's preferred modes of self- identification? (methods and tools)

• Who decides whether language should be censored in films and TV shows, and using what criteria? (ethics)

Let's finalize this chapter by developing two beautifully-formed knowledge questions based on the questions in the guide, adjusted for one of the prescribed titles published for November '21.

Title #4 is "Areas of knowledge always rely on a systematic process of trial and error to aid the production of knowledge." Discuss this claim with reference to two areas of knowledge.

As you can see, this title focuses on the "methods" of producing knowledge. Therefore, we can search among the knowledge questions related to "methods and tools."

"To what extent do the classification systems we use in the pursuit of knowledge affect the conclusions that we reach?" and "what are the implications if we do not produce knowledge in language that respects people's preferred modes of self-identification?" seem like good knowledge questions to work on.

One would choose The Natural Sciences and The Human Sciences for this title, as areas of knowledge. And based on these two areas of knowledge, and the base knowledge questions (taken from the guide) we can develop the following two KQs to be explored throughout the essay within the two AOKs:

• "To what extent can relying on a systematic process of trial and error affect the knowledge produced in chemistry?"

• "What are the implications if our systematic process of trial and error in producing knowledge in social sciences fails to meet the expectations and to match the values of the sample society?"

Hopefully, you can see the term replacements done in this example to form new knowledge questions. Remember that you can always make your own knowledge questions from scratch, or develop them based on already available knowledge questions you have explored during the course.

STRUCTURING THE ESSAY

Structuring a TOK essay might seem highly complex, but it could be pretty easy. An essential point you should never forget is that a TOK essay is not a scientific paper. You are asked to demonstrate your understanding of the course, compare and explore opposing or contrasting points of view, and reach an unbiased conclusion.

Now that you have probably chosen the right title and have hopefully formed good knowledge questions, the only thing that you need to do is to follow these three simple steps:

1. Choose your approach to the discussion. Are you planning to explore two main knowledge questions, one within each area of knowledge? Or do you intend to produce four more specific knowledge questions, for claims and counterclaims, out of those two main ones?

2. Decide if you have enough knowledge and sufficient writing skills to argue complicated real - life examples in - depth or if you would rather have a straightforward approach toward writing simple arguments for unique real - life examples.

3. Based on the above decision, you can distribute your maximum word count (1,600 words) among the introduction, AOK # 1, AOK # 2, and conclusion. Suppose

you feel less confident about your argumentation and language skills. In that case, you can focus more on your introduction, with one relatable personal example, and on your conclusion paragraph, allocating 300 – 350 words to each. Or you can allocate more, around 1,100 – 1,200 words in total, to your arguments for both areas of knowledge and leave the rest for the introduction and conclusion paragraphs, providing you feel confident about your writing and arguments.

Through the following examples, you will have a better understanding of how to choose your approach and how to structure your essay based on a given prescribed title. I warn you not to copy any of the sentences, or structures, used in these examples since the IB does not tolerate plagiarism, and your essay will be penalized. Student 1 has chosen the title "Are disputes over knowledge claims within a discipline always resolvable? "and has decided to collectively allocate (a total of) fewer than 400 words to the introduction and conclusion parts. This student has chosen four real - life examples, two for the claim and two for the counterclaim. The following is a part of the main body of this essay:

"The rigorous nature of the scientific method, ensures that data collected from experimentation can validate, refute and ... Discovery of additional empirical data from ... In Physics, the XXX view did not adhere to the new evidence and was rejected. In Psychology, the empirical evidence did

not cohere to either view and hence the conflicting claims ..."

Though personal biases or emotion may come into play, ... experimental findings render a theory useless by removing its explanatory power ... which is justified true belief. "

This essay was awarded a mark of 10/10 and is considered an accomplished essay.

Student 2 has chosen the title "The importance of establishing incontrovertible facts is overestimated. Most knowledge deals in ambiguity, "and has allocated around 450 words, collectively, to the introduction and conclusion parts. This student has also chosen four real - life examples. The following is a part of the main body of this essay:

"In the natural sciences, analytical facts in the form of definitions ... For example, scientists are divided over whether to classify ... which affects whether they focus on biomedical or psychological research to find treatments ...

In History, even where factual details of an event can be disputed, there is in general minimally a consensus ... An example of this would be the case of ... A reasonable historian will not defy the entire historical community and overwhelming evidence and ... will not be a historical debate, which is how historical knowledge is produced. "

This essay was awarded a mark of 8/10, is considered an example of a good essay, and the discussion is focused on the title, and pertinent points are made.

Student 3 has chosen the title "Disinterestedness is essential in the pursuit of knowledge, "and different parts of the essay are hard to be distinguished clearly. The introduction part blends into body 1 after 230 words, and the last paragraph, assumably the conclusion part, is made of 165 words. The student has decided to allocate the remaining 1,111 words to the arguments in the main body of the text. This way of structuring a TOK essay results in a high mark if the student has high writing skills and analytical abilities, which was a mistake in the case of this essay. The following is a part of the main body of the essay:

"I need to explore how disinterestedness can contribute in the pursuit of knowledge before I can conclude whether disinterestedness is essential or not. The distinguishing attribute … which means that other people that repeat the experiment need to confirm the results from the first experiment … However, many scientists and professors in universities repeated … Clearly, the scientific method has made disinterestedness an important factor in determining whether a scientific law can be produced from an experiment for good reason …

Although disinterestedness can contribute greatly to both the natural sciences and the human sciences, how does the way the knowledge is pursued affect ... "

This essay was awarded a mark of 6/10 and is considered satisfactory. The examiner has commented that the essay starts well but lacks analysis as it progresses. The last word of advice is that, although having few typos and minor grammatical errors do not affect your mark, it is better not to have them as everyone these days uses word editors with AIs checking every word and every sentence.

REAL - LIFE EXAMPLES

Although there is the word "theory "in TOK (theory of knowledge), it has been designed to have, and to create, a more practical approach to knowledge and learning. Therefore, every concept should be argued and explored through real - life examples (RLEs) or real - life situations (RLSs). And finding viable real - life examples is the essential first step to writing an excellent, good, or even satisfactory TOK essay.

Finding real - life examples may seem very scary, but it can be easier than you think. A word of advice: please avoid complex math or physics examples (if possible), as not all examiners are math/physics teachers.

The first RLE that you need is for the introduction part, a very simple personal experience. Let's say you have chosen the title "areas of knowledge are most useful in combination with each other, "and you intend to define the keywords and briefly explain the title in your introduction. Just remember that in your basketball team, you had the knowledge of the defense, and your teammate had the knowledge of scoring, or you could do your friend's makeup, and she could pick some good outfit for you for that party. You might want to be more relevant to the title and more sophisticated by telling the story of how you and your teammates contributed to each other's work in developing a project for

RoboCupJunior, and you could pull that off. Any little experience you have had throughout your life can be used as an excellent explanatory real - life example for the introduction. Like the writer's "hook, "your introduction part in general, and the real - life example you bring from your personal experiences, show that you had a good grasp of the title, which attracts the reader's attention (the examiner) at the beginning of the essay.

As for more complex real - life examples for the body of your essay to support your arguments, you should do more research. And it can be effectively done by following these three steps: If you have chosen the title "statistics conceal as much as they reveal, "and you intend to find real - life examples within The Natural Sciences:

1. Choose the discipline that you know best in Natural Sciences, which can be Biology (for some of you).

2. Now find an example by googling ""number of ""healthy ""and you may come across a study on "Number of healthy years of life: countries compared."

3. At this point, simply analyse the study and its statistics that show life expectancy in men and women in different countries without much

explanation about the causes and reasons behind these numbers.

You now have your real - life example to argue that statistics reveal and conceal at the same time.

We will go through some other real - life examples, taken from real assessed TOK essays, to shed more light on this issue, but before that, we should talk about research skills a bit.

Research skills is one of the ATL (approaches to learning) skills you learn and master throughout the Diploma Program. You learn how to use quotation marks, how to use keywords, which links you should trust, and what websites you should avoid while doing your online research. You can also go through the academic/scientific database of magazines and articles stored in your school's library to find all the best real - life examples you need.

Now, assuming you know how to search for viable real - life examples and you have all the necessary resources at your disposal, let's bring some real - life examples.
One student had chosen the title "Are disputes over knowledge claims within a discipline always resolvable? "and has found the example of the dispute over different models of the Earth for the argument pro the title, in Physics. This student has compared the Models of the Earth suggested by Cassini and Newton and has explored

how the scientists eventually resolved the dispute. They have also compared the Copenhagen interpretation with the Many - worlds interpretation of Feynman's double - slit experiment and has explored how this dispute was never settled, to argue against the title.

This student has brought excellent real - life examples and explored the arguments throughout these examples masterfully. As a result, their essay was awarded a mark of 10/10. Another student had chosen the title "Robust knowledge requires both consensus and disagreement. "This student has chosen different Historical Schools and Global Warming as real - life examples. Although these are good topics to explore "consensus "and "disagreement, "they are not specific examples. A real - life example, first should be a specific example where the title (question) can be explored, based on the knowledge that the given example has produced. Then it should also be taken from real life and not be fictional.

As expected, unfortunately, the student could not bring robust arguments and "has only really addressed half of the title. This essay was awarded a mark of 5/10.

It is crucial to spend as much time as you need to find the most suitable and viable real - life examples to work with, and from which you can develop your arguments.

It is always said that a professional photographer can take amazing photos using an old amateur camera. This does not apply to writing a TOK essay. Even the most experienced TOK educator cannot develop excellent arguments relating to irrelevant real - life examples. And the photographer example here was misleading and not relevant to the title of the discussion ; therefore, a lousy RLE !

INTRODUCTION

One of the definitions of the word "introduction "is "a person's first experience of a subject or thing. "This definition strictly applies to the TOK essay. Your introduction paragraph is the examiner's first experience of reading your essay. Therefore, if it catches the examiner's eye, the person reading tens of essays in a couple of days, they will read the rest of the essay more attentively and might actually enjoy reading your text.

Writing the introduction might be the easiest part of writing a TOK essay. As usual, you just need to follow these three simple steps:

1. Find the keywords in the title and define them, referencing a dictionary (some frown upon dictionary definitions), and elaborate based on your own understanding. Imagine you have chosen the title "within areas of knowledge, how can we differentiate between change and progress? "The main keywords are "change "and "progress. "So, you simply bring the definitions from a dictionary and add a few more details to show you have understood them well, or you can define them both according to your comprehensive understanding.

2. Now, briefly explain the difference between "change "and "progress "through a personal experience, a real - life example. Maybe you changed your sleeping and studying habits quite a few times, but the results were still the same, and you continued to receive the same marks. On the other hand, when you shifted your focus and concentrated more on one task, progress was made, and you saw much better results. You can surely find many examples like this in your life.

3. To complete the introduction, you may want to introduce the AOKs that you will explore and briefly explain your approach. Finishing the paragraph with a viable general knowledge question derived from the title would be a good touch, too.

Let's write an introduction paragraph for the title "Knowledge gained through direct experience is powerful but problematic" shall we?

In this sample introduction paragraph, which is quite long due to the approach chosen while structuring the essay, you will see how you can introduce, explain and expand the title by defining its keywords and personal real - life examples.

"We gain knowledge through life experiences and education. One might consider education an "indirect "way of experiencing, as educators transfer their knowledge through a systematic process to their students. This process is, to some extent, controlled, and the outcomes are already predicted. However, due to the preliminary nature of formal education and the involuntary nature of acquiring knowledge at schools, students tend to adjourn the actualization of their knowledge. It explains why, in most cases, the knowledge gained through formal education is not very powerful. On the other hand, first-hand experiences leave a powerful mark on the individual's learning process, and the knower tends to carry that knowledge for the rest of their life. However, there is a downside to this way of knowing, and that is the feeling of authority and dominance, which can cause problems. The knower, who gains knowledge through direct experience, mistakes the extent of their knowledge with the entirety of knowledge in that area, and acting upon such belief may result problematically. Such repercussions might not be imminent for everyone and in every case. I, for one, clearly remember the day that I learned, the hard way, how hard a basketball can hit your face bouncing back when you throw it to a wall. I had already learned about Newton's laws of motion, but nothing was mentioned about the pain. The way I gained knowledge through direct experience made it powerful and not problematic. In this essay, I will compare the knowledge gained through direct and indirect experiences and explore the strength of these two types of knowledge.

The possibilities of them being problematic, within the AOKs of Physics and Economics, by exploring the knowledge question "to what extent do life experiences make us feel autonomous of formal education?"

The following sample introduction is taken from one of the assessed works. This student has chosen to define the keywords without explicitly mentioning them or referring to a dictionary for the title "Are disputes over knowledge claims within a discipline always resolvable? "They have also not felt the need to write the knowledge question, yet introduced their approach to the discussion excellently, and the essay was awarded a mark of 10/10.

"Disputes over knowledge claims within disciplines constantly arise as man constantly pushes ... Discussing whether disputes over knowledge claims are always resolvable would shed more light on ... In this essay, theoretical and practical disputes will be discussed. Theoretical disputes are differing knowledge claims ... Practical disputes refer to ... ' Resolvable ' is the act of dismissing or ... In this essay, the discipline of Physics from the Natural Sciences and the discipline of Psychology from the Human Sciences will be compared and contrasted ... Theoretical disputes may be resolved using evidence ... The scientific method is a systematic process in which ... This then leads to either the abolishment, strengthening or..."

In summary, try to introduce your approach to the discussion in a concise, mildly detailed, and informative way, and be careful not to write overly academically or scientifically.

ARGUMENTS

A TOK essay is basically an argumentative essay with a twist ; you will not prove your point. One would think that such a definition makes a TOK essay a comparative one, which is not entirely correct either. To write a TOK essay, the student compares their views pro and against the title, without trying to have a strong opinion or prove a point. In summary, you should mildly argue both to agree and to disagree with the title statement/question to show your "clear awareness and evaluation of different points of view."

After structuring the essay, forming knowledge questions, finding viable real - life examples, and writing the introduction, it is time to develop your arguments. Imagine the chosen title is "avoiding bias seems a commendable goal, but this fails to recognize the positive role that bias can play in the pursuit of knowledge." You can follow these three steps and develop your arguments for your claim and counterclaim to explore within the areas of knowledge:

1. Your claim should be pro the title statement ; although some say it is better to claim against the title and then go against what we have claimed, I would instead suggest a simpler and easier - to - explain approach. For the title mentioned above, you should first explain while bias might be distracting from a big - picture view in an area of

42

knowledge (e.g., History), it can also focus the attention on a particular event and make the scientists (historians) dig deeper to find more "truth "about that specific event. Then, in the second paragraph, you go the other way around, claiming (as the counterclaim) that bias doesn't always encourage knowledge producers (historians) to dig deeper and might give them a self - righteous scientific attitude.

2. You bring your real - life example, which could be the "Gallipoli Campaign "or "the "Attack "on Pearl Harbour "within the AOK of History. Then you explain how Turkish historians see this event as a victory over "evil "ANZAC and let go of the "truth "behind the participation of Australians and New Zealanders, which is a positive role played by bias to make the historian find every little detail of what happened those days to the Ottoman army, and as the result, advance knowledge. This is the same for the view of pro - America or anti - America historians on Pearl Harbour events.

3. Now, it is time to argue that, for instance, in reporting "The Holocaust, "most historians only try to prove that it happened, while some like Harry Elmer Barnes totally deny it, and there isn't really any pursuit of knowledge. This is how bias can be an obstacle in the pursuit of knowledge.

In other areas of knowledge like The Natural Sciences, you can argue that bias can help advance knowledge, as Einstein's persistence against "Quantum Mechanics "made him contribute significantly to the same field. On the other hand, avoiding bias is still a commendable goal at times, as it might not always play a positive role in advancing knowledge. For instance, Linus Pauling, one of the most outstanding chemists in history, made a mistake in presenting the DNA model. He was not as persistent (biased) as the abovementioned genius.

The following examples show good argumentation in a TOK essay.

This student had chosen the title "The production of knowledge is always a collaborative task and never solely a product of the individual." And this is how they have formed the claims and counterclaims:

"In accordance with the statement in the area of knowledge of the natural sciences the vast majority of discoveries and production of knowledge come from collaborative work amongst scientist sometimes of different disciplines in order to share their knowledge.

"...A counter claim to this in the natural sciences could be that there is an element of the production of knowledge that is down to the work of an individual.

... A counter claim to the initial statement is that it can be suggested that knowledge does not have to be produced collaboratively but can be produced on an individual basis. This is can be seen in the area of knowledge of the arts. Creating fictional stories can be considered the production of knowledge by an individual ...

... A further counter claim would be that knowledge can often begin with an individual's ideas but then this knowledge is furthered through the help of others. This counter claim can be seen through the importance of shared knowledge within the area of knowledge of the arts. This can be seen in the domain of music within the area of knowledge of the arts, through the example of songwriters. "

This essay was awarded a mark of 10/10.

In another example, the student had chosen "The importance of establishing incontrovertible facts is overestimated. Most knowledge deals in ambiguity "as the title and this is how they have argued the claims and counterclaims:

"... The way historians evaluate sources is reliant on factors such as the prejudices of the historian's own time period, which will determine what facts are identified based on those sources. Thus, what a

historian extracts from a range of credible sources and considers to be fact can differ. For instance ...

In the natural sciences, although there is a greater emphasis on the need for empirical evidence, some theories allow for certain types of facts to be essentially ambiguous. Based on such theories, we ***must*** accept that we can never truly know certain facts."

This essay is considered a good essay and was awarded a mark of 8/10 by the examiner. In conclusion, bringing a "courtroom analogy "(used by many, over and over again), the student should act as both the attorney and the prosecutor (confusing legal titles), trying to free the title and then send it to prison. In the end, the student acts as a very irresponsible judge, with an ambiguous verdict (which will be discussed in the conclusion chapter), to show that they have carefully listened to and understood both opposing points of view, and are clearly aware of them.

CONCLUSION

Unlike scientific papers or other essays, you do not have to "reach a conclusion "per se. The student should conclude that while the title statement is, to some extent, true, at the same time, it might not apply to all real - life situations. As an example, you can follow these three steps to write the conclusion for the title "Labels are a necessity in the organization of knowledge, but they also constrain our understanding: "1Write the concluding statement. "In conclusion, to what extent do labels restrain our understanding largely depends on the nature of the knowledge that label categorizes... "2Explain each side of the statement. "Labels play a crucial role in organizing knowledge in some AOKs while ... The delivered message may not be clear enough and might mislead the audience... "3Apply the explanations to the AOKs. "In AOK # 1, labels are necessary for categorizing knowledge while ... The message labels deliver in AOK # 2 may convince the receiver of the knowledge about the entirety of... "The abovementioned example shows you how to form and develop your conclusion paragraph. Remember to avoid reaching strong and solid conclusions, pro or against the title statement/question. As it was said before, a TOK essay is not a scientific paper. While it has the characteristics of both comparative and argumentative essays, it is not exactly either of these two. Therefore, the conclusion part of a TOK essay should not be written in the same way as those types of essays. The following examples are taken from assessed works of the students to show you how not to take a side in the conclusion paragraph. "As reflected on in this essay, we need both consensus and disagreement to gain robust knowledge, given my definition of the concept. ""It has been seen, the solidification and or destabilisation of knowledge is dependent on the circumstance and the effect the solidification or destabilisation has on our knowledge. ""In conclusion, due to the objective nature of the natural sciences, it is generally preferred that we have as many incontrovertible facts from experimentation as possible. Nonetheless, there are occasions where it is not necessary to have agreed factual evidence for a theory because it is explanatorily powerful and coherent with other proven facts. "I want you to pay attention to these keywords and phrases "we need both, ""given my definition of, ""is dependent on the circumstance, ""it is generally preferred, "and "there are occasions where. "As you can see, all these students have tried not to take a stance and they've mildly agreed or disagreed, while comparing different points of view. "There is clear awareness and evaluation of different points of view. "You can see this sentence in the assessment instrument for an excellent essay. Similar sentences can be found in the descriptors for good and satisfactory essays. In conclusion, I cannot emphasize enough the importance of impartiality in acknowledging and evaluation of different points of view in the TOK course and, of course, in writing a TOK essay.

CHAPTER 3: THE TOK EXHIBITION

ASSESSMENT

TOK essay is the internal assessment component, with 1/3 (33 %) weighting. The exhibition is also marked out of 10 marks.

You create an exhibition of three objects that link to one of the 35 "IA prompts." Your exhibition will be marked out of 10 by your TOK teacher (and moderated by the IB).

Before getting into how to create a TOK exhibition, understanding the prompts and the development process, let's review the steps:

• You will choose one of the 35 IA prompts.

• You will choose three "objects "for your exhibition.
• You will write a maximum of 950 words (in total) of commentary on the objects.

Explanations:

• The IA prompts are a set of 35 high - level knowledge questions, provided by the IB in the TOK Guide, presented to the students by their TOK teacher.

• TOK Exhibition Objects are three physical or digital (images) objects, connected to one of the themes (core or optional), and linked to the chosen prompt.

• Commentary is the text describing each object and its specific real - world context, justifying its inclusion in the exhibition, and its links to the prompt.

There are also some important points to keep in mind:
• Each student must select just one IA prompt.

• Each student is required to produce a single exhibition file.

• Each student must create an individual exhibition. Group work is not accepted.

• The 950 - word count includes the written commentary. It does not include "texts on/within objects, "acknowledgments, references, or bibliography.

• The exhibition file must include: an exhibition title, clearly indicating the chosen IA prompt, Images of three objects, a typed commentary on each object, and appropriate citations and references. The following chart shows the criteria based on which the TOK exhibition is assessed:

Does the exhibition successfully show how TOK manifests in the world around us?					
Excellent 9-10	**Good** 7-8	**Satisfactory** 5-6	**Basic** 3-4	**Rudimentary** 1-2	**0**
The exhibition clearly identifies three objects and their specific real-world contexts. Links between each of the three objects and the selected IA prompt are clearly made and well-explained. There is a strong justification of the particular contribution that each individual object makes to the exhibition. All, or nearly all, of the points are well-supported by appropriate evidence and explicit references to the selected IA prompt.	The exhibition identifies three objects and their real-world contexts. Links between each of the three objects and the selected IA prompt are explained, although this explanation may lack precision and clarity in parts. There is a justification of the contribution that each individual object makes to the exhibition. Many of the points are supported by appropriate evidence and references to the selected IA prompt.	The exhibition identifies three objects, although the real-world contexts of these objects may be vaguely or imprecisely stated. There is some explanation of the links between the three objects and the selected IA prompt. There is some justification for the inclusion of each object in the exhibition. Some of the points are supported by evidence and references to the selected IA prompt.	The exhibition identifies three objects, although the real-world contexts of the objects may be implied rather than explicitly stated. Basic links between the objects and the selected IA prompt are made, but the explanation of these links is unconvincing and/or unfocused. There is a superficial justification for the inclusion of each object in the exhibition. Reasons for the inclusion of the objects are offered, but these are not supported by appropriate evidence and/or lack relevance to the selected IA prompt. There may be significant repetition across the justifications of the different objects.	The exhibition presents three objects, but the real-world contexts of these objects are not stated, or the images presented may be highly generic images of types of object rather than of specific real-world objects. Links between the objects and the selected IA prompt are made, but these are minimal, tenuous, or it is not clear what the student is trying to convey. There is very little justification offered for the inclusion of each object in the exhibition. The commentary on the objects is highly descriptive or consists only of unsupported assertions	The exhibition does not reach the standard described by the other levels or does not use one of the IA prompts provided.
Possible characteristics					
Convincing Lucid Precise	Focused Relevant Coherent	Adequate Competent Acceptable	Simplistic Limited Underdeveloped	Ineffective Descriptive Incoherent	

WHERE TO START

Although the first step seems to be choosing the IA prompt, which the IB TOK Guide "officially "suggests, I think it's better to start by choosing your favourite theme. And how can you find your favourite theme? Find out what your favourite subject is ; literature, business, economics, politics, history, philosophy, psychology, social sciences, biology, computer science, chemistry, design, physics, sports, mathematics, arts, and many more subjects that IB schools offer. I don't need to tell you which theme each object is connected to ; you can easily ask your TOK teacher if you do not already know.

Why do I suggest starting by choosing the theme? Because of this part of the TOK Guide, "It is strongly recommended that students base their exhibition on one of the themes (the core theme or one of the optional themes). This can be an extremely useful way to help students narrow down their choice of objects and give a focus to their exhibition. "Also, choosing a prompt that matches a theme is easier than matching a theme (that you may not know well) to an already chosen IA prompt.

Before moving on to the next step, which is choosing the IA prompt, let's see what a TOK exhibition object can be, as the TOK Guide says:

"The objects may be digital rather than physical objects. For example, students could include a photograph of an object, such as a historical treaty, where it would not be practical/possible for them to exhibit the physical object. Students may also use digital objects such as a tweet by a political leader. However, they must be specific objects that have a specific real - world context — objects that exist in a particular time and place (including virtual spaces). They may be objects that the student has created themselves, but they must be pre - existing objects rather than objects created specifically for the purposes of the exhibition."

The Guide also emphasizes that "the specific real - world context of each object is extremely important. "IB's example is also very clarifying. The Guide clears that the photo of your baby brother has a real - world context, whereas a generic photo of a baby (downloaded from the internet) does not. You can also use the image or the digital work of yours ; however, it should be done beforehand and not be specifically created/prepared for your TOK exhibition.

Examples of the diverse kinds of objects students could select include the following:

• A tweet from the President of the United States

• An image of the painting Guernica by Pablo Picasso

• The student's own extended essay (EE)

• A basketball used by the student during their physical education lessons

• The graphic novel The Colour of Earth by Kim Dong Hwa

• A painting that the student created in their DP visual arts course

• A refillable water bottle provided to each student in a school as part of a sustainability initiative

• A news article from the popular website Buzzfeed

• A photograph of the student playing in an orchestra

And a final word of advice about the exhibition objects is that although you must exhibit three objects, I strongly suggest that you choose five potential objects in the beginning. In the process of developing the commentaries for the object, you will find out that one or two of the objects do not perfectly match the IA prompt or the theme, or even their real - world context is not what it seemed in the beginning. So, choose five objects first.

CHOOSING THE IA PROMPT

First, read all 35 IA prompts one by one and form an opinion about them. Many of the prompts may be hard to understand, seem repetitive, or may not even make sense. If you face such feelings, do not doubt yourself because you might be absolutely right.

Regardless of all the help that you may have, I urge you to go through the following three steps: • Read all 35 IA prompts once, think about them, and form an opinion about each. • Shortlist the ones you like more (or dislike less). • Repeat the process until you have your top 3. At this point, if you successfully go through these three steps, you have three IA prompts to choose from. And don't forget that you have already chosen your favourite theme.

Now try to understand each IA prompt's connection to your theme, and the "chosen "one will emerge. It is still possible that you cannot be sure which one is the best for you to create your exhibition based on it. It is totally fine, and you can ask for help from your teacher, your classmates, or anyone with TOK knowledge.

You are not alone after all, as IB recommends that a total of 8 teaching hours should be allocated to the exhibition task by the TOK teacher. The teacher should explain the process, requirements, and prompts and initiates discussions among students. Although students are not permitted to present a group exhibition, nobody has forbidden them from brainstorming ideas and helping each other understand the IA prompts and the process. Now, hopefully, you have an IA prompt that you are happy with, as it matches your chosen theme, and you can find viable objects for, and we can continue to see how to choose great objects for your TOK Exhibition.

HOW TO CHOOSE THE OBJECTS

It is crucial to know what to choose and, more importantly, what not to choose. Do not choose concepts or methods, surely these are not "objects. "Instead of choosing your "Biology IA "or methods that you used, choose the device (s) that you used or (maybe) the test result sheet (s). Instead of choosing a NASA program or mission, choose the (official) tweets or news about the programs and missions. Above all, do not choose anything generic, be specific. Although you can download photos from the internet, you can absolutely not use stock images.

The following examples give you a better understanding of "good "and "bad "objects for the TOK exhibition.

This student had chosen the IA prompt "how is current knowledge shaped by its historical development? "and "Knowledge and Technology "as the connected theme. However, unfortunately they have chosen very generic objects that resulted in a mark of 3/10. The student has chosen the images of "a stone tablet, ""a letter "and "a laptop "as their objects. Examiner's comments read, *"another key weakness of this exhibition is that the objects selected are overly generic. Rather than generic objects such as "a laptop, "the student needed to identify objects that have a specific real - world context — objects that exist in a particular time and place."*

"Another student has chosen the first IA prompt "what counts as knowledge? "and has connected to the core theme of "Knowledge and The Knower, "with the most generic "objects "possible. Clearly, they didn't invest any time into creating the TOK exhibition, that resulted in a mark of 1/10. They have chosen "humans, ""fire "and "food, "and the objects are presented by some randomly downloaded images from the internet, which could be considered the most general concepts, and clearly a total opposite of what is expected from a TOK exhibition. The examiner's comments read, *"a key issue is that the three objects included in this exhibition are not specific objects, but instead are highly generic images, for example, "food. "The commentary on each of the three objects is also highly descriptive and has very little relevance to TOK. This exhibition demonstrates barely any engagement with the TOK prompt and demonstrates minimal understanding of how TOK manifests in the world around us."*

Contrary to the above examples, two students have masterfully explored their chosen IA prompts within the connected themes, by choosing precisely handpicked objects. One of these students has chosen "Starbucks holiday cup, ""(their) Chinese - English translation dictionary "and "Billie Holiday's song Strange Fruit "for the prompt "What challenges are raised by the dissemination and/or communication of knowledge? "connected to the theme "Knowledge and Language. "They have also titled their exhibition "Subtext and

Connotation. "This student's exhibition is awarded a mark of 10/10, with the examiner's comments highlighting, "the student has clearly identified three specific objects and has effectively linked each one to the selected prompt. There is also a strong justification for the selection of each object."

Another successful student had chosen the prompt "Does some knowledge belong only to particular communities of knowers? "The student hasn't explicitly specified the theme. However, clear connections to the core theme "Knowledge and The Knower "and the optional theme of "Knowledge and Language "can be seen by choice of the prompt and throughout the commentaries. A novel "Things Fall Apart by Chinua Achebe, "A music CD "Rapper's Delight by The Sugar Hill Gang "and the image of a pink knitted hat, AKA "Pussycat "are their objects. This precise and processed choice of objects helped the student's exhibition to be awarded a mark of 9/10 as the examiner expresses their opinion, *"the student clearly identifies three objects and their real - world contexts and then makes clear links between the objects and the TOK prompt. Each of the individual objects is shown to make an interesting contribution to the exhibition."*

As you can see through these examples, I cannot emphasize enough how important it is for you to choose objects that are **specific, personal, and with real - world context**. This means that:

• The objects must belong to a specific time and space, and preferably a person or a culture.

• The objects must have a personal connection with you, such as you own them or have used them or similar connections.

• The objects must be used in a specific context in the real world, which means not to be of conceptual nature, such as an idea or a plan.

There are a couple of more points for you to keep in mind at the time of choosing your TOK exhibition objects:

• Keep it simple: As long as your teacher does not belong to the culture of "the more, the merrier, "that means they prefer complexity and long texts over simplicity and concision, it is better to keep the objects and their titles simple.

• Be Relatable: Although this is not a must, and due to the age and probably cultural differences, the chances of you and your teacher relating to the same objects are low, still, try not to choose something very hard for your teacher to relate to.

• Make it Beautiful: Nobody has ever asked for the objects or the images to be beautiful ; still, it is an exhibition after all, and no "ugly "items bring good reception for an exhibition.

Considering that you already have your five potential objects ready, it's time to start writing the commentaries. In the next section of this chapter, we'll discuss what to include or not to in your commentaries and how to write the texts.

WRITING THE COMMENTARIES

The TOK Exhibition needs a unique style of text; commentary. In writing the commentaries of the objects, you can also add a short introduction and conclusion, although it is not mandatory. It means you can structure the text for your exhibition in a combination of introduction, commentaries, and conclusion.

Commentaries, which are explanations of the objects, are mandatory and cannot be removed. The introduction and conclusion parts are, on the other hand, optional. Strongly based on the prompt, themes, objects, and your writing approach, and in some cases, your TOK teacher's preferences, the "Introduction "and "conclusion "parts can be included or removed from the exhibition's text. Therefore, as there's no strict structure for the exhibition text, I will explain how to write and include the "introduction "and "conclusion "parts, along with the commentaries of the objects, in case you prefer to add them, or it is asked of you to do so by your TOK teacher.

Before we dive into writing, there are some points that you should keep in mind:

• Introduce your exhibition shortly (if applicable).

• Contextualize: clearly identify the objects and effectively link each to the selected prompt.

- Strongly justify the selection of each object.
- If possible, try to compare your objects.

- Have a holistic view of your exhibition.

- Do not cross 950 words.

WRITING THE INTRODUCTION

If you intend to have an "introduction, "keep it short. Briefly introduce your exhibition by clearly identifying the selected prompt and the theme and explaining why you have chosen these particular objects. Before I bring you examples of excellent and average exhibitions, I must warn you not to copy any of the sentences or structures used in these examples since the IB does not tolerate plagiarism, and your essay will be penalized. An example of a good introduction is the following text from a student's exhibition that was awarded a mark of 10/10, with examiner's expressing their satisfaction for the inclusion of the introduction part (although it was not required):

"The TOK prompt I have selected is: "What challenges are raised by the dissemination and/or communication of knowledge? "This exhibition explores this prompt by reflecting on knowledge and language, and more specifically on whether subtext and connotation always create confusion rather than help us to communicate knowledge. The language we use in our everyday lives can often be interpreted many different ways by different people, depending on their cultural background, beliefs, ideologies, affiliations, personal experiences etc. In particular it seems that subtext and connotation can be particularly challenging as they are often only

recognised by people that share some particular knowledge or experiences, and it seems that they can easily be interpreted very differently by different people which can cause confusion and hinder communication of knowledge. "

Contextualization

You must clearly identify the objects by describing them in relevant detail. The reader should be able to understand what each object is and how it functions in the real world. You must also effectively link each object to the IA prompt by explaining its connection. This is how one successful student has contextualized their object, a "Starbucks holiday cup "chosen for the above prompt:

"This cup was used by Starbucks in 2017 and was controversial because some people viewed the symbol of the two hands holding hands on the cup as a sign that Starbucks was promoting a homosexual agenda, because they saw the cups as having an LGBT subtext. "

Their exhibition was awarded a mark of 10/10.

Justification

Another aspect of the commentary, which is requested, is for the text to strongly justify the selection of the object. You should convince the reader why you have chosen each object and how their placement helps exhibit the IA prompt in the real world. The following is a good example for justification of the object "fishing spears "(used by the aboriginals in Australia), chosen for the prompt "Are some types of knowledge more useful than others? ":

"I chose this object carefully to help show that both content - based and procedural knowledge are important and useful depending on the situation, and that sometimes actually procedural knowledge is far more useful. "

Comparison

Although comparison between the objects is not required and is also a bit risky, you should know that if you can make a brief but effective link between two objects by comparing them, it may help you get a better mark, as we read in the examiner's comment for one "satisfactory "exhibition, **"in this particular case the student also makes links between their three objects, which is not required but can be a valid way to help justify the inclusion of an object. "**

Holistic View

You must have a holistic view of your exhibition. It means that while you focus on writing great commentaries for each object, you should also pay attention to the entire text as a whole. You must pay attention to all the places where you discuss an object, an approach, or the IA prompt. For instance, if you mention any of the objects in your "introduction, "the way that you explain the object in its commentary should match that first introduction. It is the same if you link to an object in the commentary of another object. In general, all your approaches and explanations in all parts of the text should match in concept and style.

I will end this chapter by attracting your attention to the mistakes that may cost you marks by bringing reasons for reducing marks from examiners.' comments. You can read these comments carefully to avoid making the same mistakes and to be able to achieve higher marks:

"The main issue with this example is that barely any links are made between the objects and the prompt ... the student would need to keep referring back to that prompt ... throughout their commentaries on their objects ... It is important that students make the real - world context of the objects clear, but this goes too far and devotes almost all of the commentary to simply describe the details of the object. "2/10

"The student has focused on how technology has changed over time, rather than using examples relating to technology to focus on how knowledge has changed over time. Because of this the response lacks relevance to the prompt. Another key weakness of this

exhibition is that the objects selected are overly generic. "3/10

"This response does not score more highly because while there is some explanation of the links between the objects and the prompt, this explanation is underdeveloped rather than well - explained. The response is significantly under the word count and would require further development and justification of points in order to achieve a higher mark."6/ 10

"The justification needs to be stronger and more convincing and the points more precise if this piece of work is to achieve a mark in the top band, particularly for the second and third objects." 710

"The explanation does lack precision and clarity in places. "8/10

"The reason that this exhibition was only awarded 9/10 rather than 10/10 is that there is some repetition in the discussion of the different objects, and some of the points were not completely clear. "9/10

CHAPTER 4: TEN GRADE-A TOK ESSAYS

EXAMPLE 1

<u>Title:</u> Is there solid justification for regarding knowledge in the natural sciences more highly than knowledge in another area of knowledge? Discuss with reference to the natural sciences and one other area of knowledge.

<u>Grade:</u> A

<u>Author:</u> Anonymous

<u>Session:</u> May 2022

Is there solid justification for regarding knowledge in the natural sciences more highly than knowledge in another area of knowledge? Discuss with reference to the natural sciences and one other area of knowledge

Word count: 1584

When I was deciding between a Chemistry and Geography major to apply for university last year, many of my peers, and especially my parents, told me to choose Chemistry, as they regarded the subject to be more "respectable" than Geography. As a proud Geo-nerd, I was quite appalled at their responses, as I regard Geography to be equally interesting and respectable to Chemistry. From life-saving medical technology to the computer I am using to type this essay, it is no question that knowledge in Chemistry, and the natural sciences overall, has significantly helped humanity achieve the convenient lifestyle that we have today. However, it is not to say that knowledge in Geography and the human sciences have not contributed to society's progress, either. Economic laws, psychological therapy, and other branches of the Human sciences have all helped society develop in one way or another.

My parents believe that there is solid justification to regard the natural sciences more highly than the human sciences, and would undoubtedly agree with this essay title. They justified Chemistry as being more "reputable" than Geography by saying that it not only has better job opportunities but also more impact on society, using the example of Liquid Crystal Displays (LCDs) as a significant innovation from Chemistry. While I do value LCDs and use them daily, I justify Geography as being equally respectable due to its unique position as a bridge between the natural and human sciences. As I aim to pursue a career in sustainability, I strongly value the environmental knowledge that Geography can give us. Although both opinions are valid, I don't believe my parent's justification is solid, as the Geo-nerd within me understands the value that knowledge in Geography holds in tackling our climate crisis. At the same time, my parents do not think my justification is solid, either, as they believe majoring in Geography will provide no positive future for me. Therefore, it can be argued that while there is justification for regarding the natural sciences more highly than the human sciences, there may be no such thing as solid justification, as individuals will have different values and perspectives that influence what they consider as "solid".

Furthermore, not only are individuals' values different, but also the scopes of the Natural Sciences and Human Sciences too: the Natural Sciences make knowledge claims on the natural world, while the Human Sciences aim to gain knowledge of human existence and behaviour. Consequently, both Areas of Knowledge (AOKs) have unique strengths that no other AOK can offer. For example, in Geography, research in environmental processes and humanity's relationship to a certain location can help us make informed decisions on how we should continue to live on our planet in a sustainable way. While Chemistry cannot offer the same, research in Green Chemistry can help us adapt or mitigate the effects of climate change by innovating new technologies to replace environmentally damaging ones. Therefore, there is no solid justification to regard knowledge in the natural sciences more highly than the human sciences, as due to their differing scopes, the human sciences offer unique knowledge claims that cannot be replaced by knowledge in the natural sciences.

In addition, while Chemistry and the Natural Sciences aim to create static knowledge to turn into laws, the Human Sciences are more concerned with understanding human behaviour at a specific point in time. Therefore, the same type of knowledge will hold a different value to both AOKs. For example, in my Geography IA, I focused on the effects of human intervention on natural vegetation patterns found at Changi Beach by measuring the volume of trash found. However, the trash found on the beach changed daily based on the weather conditions (wind blowing trash on the beach) and the extent to which beach users litter. Therefore, the data I collected varied greatly each day. From a natural scientist's perspective, such varied data would not be valuable, as it will be difficult to construct a law, which should see the same results each time. However, from a human scientist's perspective, this data is valuable, as it shows the patterns of human behaviour, which is what I was interested in researching. In this sense, there is no solid justification to regard knowledge in the natural sciences more highly than the human sciences, as an individual's perceived value of knowledge will depend on their specific inquiry or situation, which may also change over time.

It is interesting that natural scientists may not value the data I collected in my Geography IA, as I used the scientific method to create my knowledge claim, which should, in theory, make my data reliable. Both natural and human scientists use the cyclical process of the scientific method to observe, form hypotheses, carry out experiments to test and reject, or accept, hypotheses based on analysis. In addition, both AOKs utilise peer-review to ensure the knowledge being published is reliable and accurate, minimising fabrication and bias. Although peer-review can sometimes be fabricated, knowledge in both the natural and human sciences are equally subject to this. Therefore, from a non-scientific perspective, knowledge in both AOKs may be regarded as commensurate, as they are derived from the same methods that are meant to ensure reliability and validity, regardless of if they aim to achieve different types of knowledge.

However, natural scientists, or non-human scientists, may justify knowledge in the Natural Sciences more highly due to the constraints of the scientific method faced by the Human Sciences. Because the Human Sciences, such as psychology, focus on knowledge derived from experiments observing the patterns of human behaviour, there are ethical constraints on what experiments can be done. This may be argued as making knowledge in the Human Sciences less reliable or valid, as some knowledge claims cannot be directly experimented on with humans, but other animals instead. While it is questionable that by observing non-human behaviour, human scientists can gain insight into human behaviour, it is important to consider that most research articles contain an evaluation/discussion of the experiment conducted, highlighting the limitations of the study (Casey et al.). Therefore, although human scientists may use mice to generate their knowledge claim on human behaviour, they are aware of and make the limitations in the study transparent, validating their research.

Moreover, when human and natural scientists publish research and knowledge claims, the value of these studies then lie in other scientists extending or falsifying those knowledge claims. For example, I attended a lecture in the summer by a chemistry professor discussing his current research in finding a catalyst to convert carbon dioxide into an industrial feedstock. However, what intrigued me the most about his research was that it would not be feasible to use their catalyst in the real world. When I asked him why they still continue to do this research, knowing it will never be used in the industry, he responded by saying that he believes his research is useful, as he hopes scientists will use his research as the foundation for their own innovations (Hazari). Therefore, by focusing on one method of generating knowledge claims in the human sciences, such as experimentation with mice, it may provide solid justification to regard knowledge in the natural sciences more highly as it could be argued that this method of experimentation is flawed. However, by looking at the bigger picture on how knowledge claims are actually generated in both the human and natural sciences, which is by building on existing research among the scientific community, there may not be solid justification to regard knowledge in the Natural Sciences more highly, as in both sciences, a knowledge claim cannot be accepted or rejected by one experiment alone.

However, there are still people who are sceptical of knowledge in the Natural Sciences, regardless of the use of the scientific method and peer review. For example, whether we should be concerned about climate change still remains a divided issue in the general public, even though the majority of the natural science community have reached a consensus (Kamarck). While concrete scientific facts have deemed climate change to be real, this lack of faith in scientific knowledge may arise from previous personal experiences, such as encounters with fake news or conflicting beliefs, such as from religion, both of which depend greatly on the individual. This lack of faith can also stem from a lack of knowledge in the subject. In addition, although one does not believe in climate science, one may have high regard for other areas of the Natural Sciences. Therefore, it depends on the perspective of the individual, and what they chose to have faith in, in order to have solid justification to regard knowledge in the natural sciences more highly than the human sciences.

To conclude, whether there is solid justification to regard knowledge in the Natural Sciences more highly than knowledge in the human sciences depends on the individual's perspective, which will vary based on their experiences, values and current knowledge of both AOKs. However, if the Natural Sciences are regarded more highly, what will this mean for the future of interdisciplinary studies between the Natural and Human Sciences? Scientists will have to ensure that scientific research is not biased, such that knowledge in the Human Sciences holds as much value as the Natural Sciences in contributing to societal development. When I become a scientist, either working in a laboratory as a chemist or in the jungle as a Geographer, I will strive to appreciate knowledge from all AOKs and equally recognise their unique strengths.

EXAMPLE 2

<u>Title:</u> Is there a trade-off between scepticism and the successful production of knowledge?

<u>Grade:</u> A

<u>Author:</u> Anonymous

<u>Session:</u> November 2019

Scepticism is our doubt about whether or not we know something. Scepticism allows us to know what we know and what we don't. Our minds are capable of proposing unlimited kinds of knowledge claims and scepticism helps us eliminate falsehoods that lurk amongst knowledge.

The benefits people reap from scepticism is most obvious in the area of knowledge (AOK) of the natural sciences. The scientific method invites scientists to question their observations to produce knowledge. Our current knowledge of diseases being caused by infections of germs and pathogens were developed by scientists who questioned the false belief that claimed diseases are "divine retribution" to sinners. Because they were sceptical of the existing knowledge before, they formed new knowledge using better justification by conducting extensive scientific experiments that used reason, intuition, and imagination among many ways of knowing (WOKs) to justify their claims. People's urge to doubt existing knowledge is what drives knowledge in the natural sciences forward.

However, scepticism should not be carried too far, else trade-off between septicism and the successful production of knowledge will begin to emerge. The more sceptical we are, the more difficult it is to produce knowledge. There is no way to seek the absolute truth to everything or have a perfect justification of a true belief. Alternative explanations, no matter how improbable, can always be proposed. Global sceptical scenarios such as Descartes's famous claim: maybe an evil monster is deceiving me, so everything I sense could be false, questions even the most common sense knowledge. The WOKs used to justify true beliefs can always be improved, for instance, there is no perfect scientific experiment that perfectly controls all the control variables. If sceptics fail to believe the simplest ideas, they would be unable to elaborate on those ideas to create knowledge. If we try to seek proof to everything, knowledge creation could grind to a halt, because we would be spending all our efforts in proving basic facts. Over-scepticism also paralyses the sceptic when he cannot find the answer to the scepticism he might then feel disillusioned and give up on answering the question. Over-scepticism also leads to an infinite regress where proposition 1 requires the support of proposition 2 which itself requires the support of proposition 3, and so on.

I personally experienced how absolute scepticism can impede the creation of knowledge in my English Paper One mock exams. Students must write a commentary on a poem. We then have to show how the poet uses different techniques to make a point. I couldn't think of anything because I took on the absolute scepticist position. Whenever I found a literary technique such as a metaphor, I doubted whether there is actually any hidden meaning behind it. Maybe there is, maybe the writer simply meant what he meant literally, maybe... I proposed so many possibilities that it was impossible for me to prove them. Eventually, I confused myself enough to hand in a blank paper. I had limited time for the exam, and I could not afford to ask meta-knowledge questions, or else I will run out of time to answer the questions about literature. This shows that there is an opportunity cost of over-scepticism where time could be better used to answer more obvious practical questions. The more time we spend on doubting and testing a few knowledge claims, the more time we cannot spend acquiring new knowledge claims that we are less sure about.

A cut-off point for knowledge claims where beyond it we should stop being sceptical, at least until that knowledge claim appears to be problematic, seems to be necessary to mitigate such a tradeoff. Plato defined knowledge as justified true belief. This is a good cut-off point. Once a knowledge claim is a justified true belief, we should stop being sceptical because it is likely a true claim. We can and should test the justification and truthfulness of each knowledge claim. We justify knowledge using the ways of knowing;

however, there are justifications that do not justify the claims well. For instance, US President Trump's use of fallacious reasoning when he says "They're [other countries] sending us not the right people." so it makes America weak is a black and white fallacy. The logic simplifies the argument by referring immigrants as "right" or "wrong" disregarding any complexity, so this is a weak justification to his claim. Scepticism can limit the existence of this type of belief.

Although there should be cut-off points, the degree of scepticism one should hold about the justification and the truthfulness of a true belief is situational. Once I was organising an event and had to know if the number of people attending was under 40. I asked my friend and she said 73 people are attending, so I inferred that more than 40 people would attend. My friend turned out to be mistaken, 70 instead of 73 people were expected to attend. Nevertheless, I came to the right conclusion through inference from a falsehood. This real-life-situation shows that the degree of scepticism needed for each knowledge claim is situationally different. I reckoned it sensible to trust the information my friend gave me even with its potential uncertainties because it was unlikely for her to misremember 34 extra people. However, if today I were to ask "Is the number of people attending under 70?", then I should be more sceptical about her information because the margin of error is smaller in this case. There is no universally appropriate level of scepticism, since it is different situationally. The decision on the level to apply lies on the individual in situations.

Trade-offs seem to exist between scepticism and the production of knowledge in non-falsifiable AOKs. Falsifiability is the ability of a conjecture to be disproven. Because there is no straightforward way to disprove non-falsifiable AOKs such as religious knowledge systems (RKS) and ethics, answers cannot be found after one becomes sceptical. In the falsifiable AOKs, evidence that proves or disprove the doubt can be found by conducting experiments, this is not an option in non-falsifiable AOKs. One can argue in non-falsifiable AOKs, the justification of knowledge claims depends largely on faith. God exists because I have faith. Faith does not require evidence to support it. The search for evidence actually undermines faith because if one truly has faith in something, evidences are not required. The evidentialism position states that if a belief is to be counted as rational, then it must be supported by rational evidence. Taking on this position, the more sceptical one is in religion, more knowledge is disregarded due to the their insufficient evidences. Instead of guiding people to add certainty in knowledge creation and helping people eliminate falsehoods, these functions of scepticism fail in non-falsifiable AOKs. However, if one is to acknowledge that some beliefs elicit more faith than others then one can be sceptical about beliefs in religion, and scepticism can guide people in produce beliefs that elicit the most faith. For instance, two beliefs: "God is omniscient." and "Aliens are gods.", the first one is better justified because most people have more faith in it. However, this use of scepticism is possible only if evidentialism is disregarded.

The AOK of the arts is concerned with eliciting responses in people. We can be sceptical about art by questioning why we have particular responses towards an artwork. Consensus on beauty and the interpretation of shapes, colours, and sounds exists on a general level. In 1944 experimental psychologists Fritz Heider and Marianne Simmel conducted an experiment using a short animated movie involving moving geometric shapes. Despite subjects seeing only moving shapes, they had similar responses. "Most of thirty four subjects interpreted the shapes in the movie as animate characters". (Goldman, 2013) Most of them identified the triangles to be male and the circle to be female. Through this experiment, I think our common responses to things we are not taught stems from our shared cultural and biological roots. Because the experiment was conducted in the USA in 1944, in a patriarchal society, it is likely that subjects attributed the triangles, the shapes that seem to dominate the action, to men. Biologically we are wired to think in certain ways. For instance, human beings like most animals find symmetric shapes pleasing. The standard that people use to see art then comes from these shared cultural and biological roots. There is good and bad art, good art that successfully elicits particular responses, and bad art that does so badly. The objective of the literature exam I sat was to test student's ability to distinguish the quality of a piece of literary art. We can be sceptical about our feelings towards particular pieces of art, and we can question our justification of it. This is the job of art critics and they help artists produce better art by analysing which artistic strategies appeal to which specific biological and cultural factors. A healthy dose of scepticism in the arts foster knowledge production, so trade-offs need not exist.

Although different AOKs possess different characteristics, with both the natural sciences and RKS bent on seeking the truth of the world in starkly different ways, the arts seeking to elicit particular responses in people... Scepticism may seem to only work for AOKs that are falsifiable and truth-seeking, but it can aid knowledge production AOKs not concerned with truth preventing the creation of knowledge that is poorly justified. Although it is impossible to seek the truthfulness of non-falsifiable AOKs, it is possible to rate their justification. Yet, trade-offs can exist when scepticism is carried too far, but this balance depends on each situation.

EXAMPLE 3

<u>Title:</u> "Present knowledge is wholly dependent on past knowledge." Discuss this claim with reference to two areas of knowledge.

<u>Grade:</u> A

<u>Author:</u> Anonymous

<u>Session:</u> May 2019

The title above mentioned is questioning the dependence of current known information on any information investigated in the past. It is important to determine what is considered present and past. However, there is no definite answer to what is considered present and past, this can vary upon the interpretation of people. For some people present may be within a short period of time such as a couple of days, however others may consider present within a couple of years. It is important to consider at what scale present and past are interpreted and based on that answer the. Many people do not understand the extensive process of creating new knowledge in various areas of knowledge (AOK). All knowledge had to be created at a certain point and from there it was developed or added upon. In school we are often taught how the natural and artistic world around us works, but we never focus on where this information originated. We learn the formulas, theories and laws that we can equip in our everyday lives, but we never learn about their history. I can barely remember ever going in depth questioning where this knowledge we are being taught originates from. Did some scientists just make it up? Or was it based on previous findings of other scientists. The two AOKs that will be used to discuss the claim of present knowledge being wholly dependent on past knowledge are the natural sciences and the arts. This will be shown through identifying to what extent present knowledge is dependent upon past knowledge due to deductive and inductive reasoning in the natural sciences and to what extent present knowledge is independent of past knowledge through imagination in arts, with other WOKs used to support this statement.

In the natural sciences, a majority of present knowledge is more dependent on past knowledge claims due to theories being based on simplified reality or already conducted experiments. An example of this is the equation that Sir Isaac Newton constructed, $F = G \frac{Mm}{r^2}$ (Finkenstadt). Although in school we are often taught that Sir Isaac Newton 'invented' this equation, he hasn't fully invented all of the incorporated knowledge within this equation. This equation is a composite of previously created knowledge claims such as Euclidean geometry in the early 300BC (Boyer) and Campanus Nouariensis in the 13th century (Finkenstadt) proving the existence of gravity. Through deductive reasoning Newton was able to amalgamate multiple premises in order to create a conclusion, resulting in new knowledge which was beyond the scope of what society knew at the time. This indicating that although it was considered a new piece of knowledge, the foundations of the equation were based on past premises evincing the high extent to which present knowledge depends on past knowledge supporting the knowledge claim. In this situation it could even be considered that it's only an extension to the existing premises Newton based his equation on. Using the equation example, it can be observed that the combination of already known premises through deductive reasoning has proven to support the knowledge claim.

The natural sciences bring forward many different knowledge claims which were investigated throughout our rather short-known history. Due to the limited time and technology we had in our universe so far we are to this day still making new observations resulting in the creation of new knowledge. An example of this is the recently discovered (2018) sea's deepest fish, *Pseudoliparis swirei* (Breyer). With more advanced technology scientists were able to submerge deeper into the depths of the ocean. With higher resolution cameras under water, scientists were able to identify a fish living 7,500 metres under water. In the past we were unaware of such a fish. Using inductive reasoning, observations were made with following generalizations and a hypothesis to prove the validity of this knowledge claim. Inductive reasoning refers to a logical process in which premises are believed to be true and are combined to receive a specific generalization. From these generalizations scientists were able to create paradigms which followed the observations of this specific fish and its' habitat. From this example it can be seen that due to the advancement in technology, we are able to make observations that were never made before resulting in newly formed knowledge claims and extending our present knowledge. Through inductive reasoning, it can be suggested that present knowledge is wholly dependent on past knowledge because without past knowledge we would not be able to advance further in such discoveries. The generalizations that were made based upon past knowledge of the deep sea were proved to be true (Breyer) with the newly observed *Pseudoliparis swirei* behaving similar to other deep water fish such as the *Abyssobrotula Galathea* (Breyer). Using these generalizations about *Abyssobrotula Galathea* scientists were able to draw connections with the *Pseudoliparis swirei*. Using past knowledge new generalizations were made and therefore suggesting that present knowledge is wholly dependent on past knowledge. It can be speculated the fish was observed for the first time, however it has to be considered how much past knowledge was used to be able to make this observation. All the technology incorporated in this observation was based on past knowledge, the scientists were able to base their predictions on past knowledge and we were able to determine that this is the deepest living fish due to the past knowledge already available to us. Although it was a completely new observation made, the shear amount of past knowledge that was used to make this observation, it can be concluded that this observation was wholly dependent on past knowledge.

Art is often thought of as the classic artworks or music, however it covers a much larger variety of knowledge. Art can be influenced by numerous factors. The outcome of an artwork could depend upon the time period it was created, the personal preferences of the creator or could be based on a previous artwork. All artwork is different and unique in its individual way and therefore there is a knowledge question that has to be asked. If so, in what ways does artwork add to our knowledge? There are many varieties and each source their inspiration from areas. Art can both be created based on past knowledge but also can be completely independent of it. An example that supports this knowledge claim is the surrealist style created by Salvador Dali in the 1920s (Gala) is nowadays an inspiration for many artists. Modern day artists such as Julie Curtiss (Cohen), base their paintings on the aforementioned idea of surrealism. This suggests that in present knowledge, the basis of creation is extracted from past knowledge to a high extent. Even if artists are attempting to create an individual artwork, never created before, they always incorporate some sort of feature that was already used in the past (Cohen). This can vary from artist to artist and their individual inspirations, however regardless the past knowledge is incorporated in modern artworks and supports the claim of being wholly dependent on past knowledge.

On the other hand, art is a very disputed AOK as it can solely be based on an event that has not yet happened or might never happen. This leads to the question of, to what extent is art dependent on events surrounding its creation. In todays' society artwork is extremely hard to differentiate between good and bad. Some artistic theories are disregarded as having the true value of being an artwork, while some other controversial pieces of artwork are gaining recognition. Given that any individuals brain has an extensive and different imagination that is beyond what most other individuals can imagine, new artwork independent of the past can be created, resulting in potentially new knowledge being created. This statement can be true to the extent where the created artwork doesn't incorporate any past knowledge. Taken this into consideration, the possibilities are relatively limited due to the human brain being influenced by its surroundings and experiences. Without any past knowledge, the human brain is unable to base its creativity on a specific piece of information. According to a psychological paper written by David Brieber, "the human brain is unable to solely base a premises on something it has never seen before" (Brieber). With this statement, it can be further suggested that in arts, all present knowledge is wholly dependent on past knowledge due to the absence of ability to create something new. It can be argued that through intuition and imagination, humans are able to imagine something physically impossible, however the premises of this thought is still based off something the human brain has seen before. This leading back to the knowledge claim which suggests the full dependence of present knowledge on past knowledge.

In conclusion, using two AOKs it could be observed that present knowledge is significantly dependent on past knowledge however, there could be exceptions to this claim as aforementioned with deepest fish observation. It can be argued that past knowledge was used to make that observation due to the advanced technology behind the discovery. In the arts examples, some arts can be deliberately dependent upon past knowledge in order to meet the artistic style, however even newly formed art knowledge has a degree of dependency on past knowledge or else it would be unimaginable.

Works Cited

Boyer, Carl B., and Uta C. Merzbach. *A History of Mathematics*. John Wiley & Sons, 2011.

Breyer, Melissa. "Top 10 Newly Discovered Species of 2018." *TreeHugger*, 23 May 2018, www.treehugger.com/natural-sciences/top-10-newly-discovered-species-2018.html. Accessed 29 Oct. 2019.

Brieber, David, et al. "Art in Time and Space: Context Modulates the Relation Between Art Experience and Viewing Time." *PubMed Central (PMC)*, 3 June 2014, www.ncbi.nlm.nih.gov/pmc/articles/PMC4043844/. Accessed 7 Nov. 2019.

Cohen, Alina. "These Contemporary Artists Are Keeping Surrealism Alive." *Artsy*, 5 July 2019, www.artsy.net/article/artsy-editorial-artists-putting-contemporary-spin-surrealism. Accessed 30 Oct. 2019.

Finkenstadt, Dan, Ch. 13 - Gravitation. 2015. www.usna.edu/Users/physics/finkenst/homepage_files/SP211/Chapter_13.pdf. Accessed 28 Oct. 2019.

Gala, Fundació. "Salvador Dali Surrealism and Art Style | The Dalí Universe." *The Dalí Universe: Modern Art Exhibits and Sculpture*, 2016, www.thedaliuniverse.com/en/salvador-dali/surrealism. Accessed 30 Oct. 2019.

EXAMPLE 4

Title: Can there be knowledge that is independent of culture? Discuss with reference to mathematics and one other area of knowledge.

Grade: A

Author: Anonymous

Session: May 2022

Can there be knowledge that is independent of culture? Discuss with reference to mathematics and one other area of knowledge (1599 words)

"You must pray to God every day and participate in our culture's festivities," my mother often pleads to me. But since childhood, I have challenged my parents' ways of knowing in this regard, questioning the justification behind devotion to God and the celebration of culture. My parents argue that their culture enriched their "approach to learning" and experiences at school, which is why I should value culture—but to what extent is that true? Does culture really affect the knowledge we generate at school? As a mathematics and art student, I am especially intrigued by this question—how does culture impact my knowledge in these disparate fields? Firstly, culture is defined as an individual's identity, experiences, and society, such that it influences their emotion, sense perception, interpretations, and ideals. Hence, in the arts, culture impacts the knowledge an individual derives, as art often requires a direct emotional interaction. In mathematics, conversely, varying societies and thus, varying cultures, generate and apply mathematical knowledge differently. In that sense, knowledge from both areas is independent of culture, but there is more nuance that must be discussed.

Firstly, in the arts, our experiences—manifested in any form, be it, for example, sensory, inherited, or observed—heavily shape our perception, so derived knowledge is often not independent of culture. For instance, poetry analysis in Language and Literature classes is undoubtedly subjective. In Carol Ann Duffy's Politics[1], I thought...

"...how it roars, to your moral compass truth, POLITICS, POLITICS, POLITICS,"

...emphasised her purpose through repetition. As part of the culture of the course, I looked at a diverse method of knowledge creation in literature, especially immersing myself in the culture of rhetoric—which influenced the knowledge I interpreted from the line of poetry. Conversely, a friend—an avid rower—assumed it alludes to the readjustment of a boat because it mentioned a compass. As an Indian with no exposure to rowing culture, my understanding of the meaning was wildly different; our interpretations of the knowledge were dependent on culture. Then again, there is also

---
[1] See appendix for full poem.

an authority figure in the culture of education. They determine the accuracy of interpretations even though everything is subjective—my teacher offered her own opinion in the discussion, suggesting the capitalisation emphasises the author's purpose. Many classmates ignored their own interpretation—influenced by culture—and wrote down my teacher's seemingly objective response. Having said that, even my teacher's interpretation would have been influenced by her local culture dimension in education as it defines value in the arts. Ultimately, our culture influences and differentiates each individual's interpretation of art. Even the knowledge possessed and distributed by authority figures is influenced by culture.

Alternatively, there can still be an inherent level of culture-independent knowledge derived from artwork. For instance, investigating visual arts, Yves Klein's Blue Monochrome is indeed blue.

Figure 1: An individual looking at Blue Monochrome by Yves Klein (Lee)

Then again, the knowledge we possess in sense perception demonstrates that colours may not be the same for everybody—my blue could be someone else's green (Stafford). Moreover, even colour itself is influenced by culture. In Telugu, yellow is pasupu rangu, which translates to "turmeric colour." As turmeric plants are extensively used in Hindu prayers, it is apparent how our culture influences even the colours we describe. Surroundings also play a significant role—blue in Telugu translates to "sky colour", and purple is "eggplant colour".

Still, culture-independent truths to Blue Monochrome exist. The artwork consists of only one colour. It is painted on a canvas. These culture-independent statements may be accurate, but they cannot be used to generate an emotional interaction with the reader. As Murphy and J. Stephen (1996) highlight in their research thesis, the importance of Blue Monochrome and its ability to induce an emotional response in the reader lies in its societal context. It is highly sought after because of its exclusivity and monetary value in the market, which is also an authority figure. The individual, knowing Blue Monochrome's authentication by the market, is likely to generate more emotional knowledge from the piece than from only knowing it is objectively blue or that it is on a canvas. Contrarily, research from Dara Djavan Khoshdel (2012) found that the emotional response of a viewer did not vary based on an artwork's price. Nonetheless, since the relationship between the artist and the reader is often based on emotional interaction, which culture can conceivably impact, knowledge derived from visual artwork is not independent of culture. As such, individuals have varying interpretations of the knowledge generated by artwork even without the market context. Personally, when I look at Blue Monochrome, I feel a level of cosmic sensibility; the deep blue reminds me of the skies of my Indian hometown. To me, the blue represents freedom; on the day of Indian independence in 1947, my great-grandfather said the sky was bluer, the trees were greener, and the birds were in harmony. Evidently, the arts provide the deepest insights into the human condition, leading us to a nuanced understanding of ourselves. As the human condition is largely built on identity, experiences, and society, these insights—knowledge—cannot be independent of culture.

On the other hand, there may be a problem in the definition of culture itself: by defining culture as one's identity, experiences, and society, it simply becomes "all ideas of humans," effectively losing its potency. Even then, the stark discrepancy between the interpretations of artwork demonstrates how the generation of emotional knowledge through interaction is imbued with culture.

Conversely, this phenomenon is not necessarily the same in mathematics; mathematical theorems are considered to hold a priori. In that sense, if cultures precisely define a new set of obscure mathematical axioms and symbols and construct valid knowledge claims with them, it is mappable to the rest of the mathematical body of knowledge. Thus, regardless of varying mathematical approaches by cultures, the underlying calculus fundamentally is the same. Ancient Egyptian civilisations, for example, used the base-ten numeral system in 3,000 BCE (Smith and LeVeque). Conversely, the Aztecs and Mayans utilised base-twenty systems. Despite their cultures defining different axioms and symbols, the derived knowledge—calculations—from their mathematical methods was still the same. However, does mathematics exist without its interpretation? It may be true that the clichéd $1 + 1$ is 2 or that $8,000$ is $8,000$ units, but how one visualises the equation mathematically depends on their culture's interpretation of it. For instance, the Mayans and Aztecs used different symbols to depict 8,000 (Figure 2).

(a) Aztec

(b) Mayan

Figure 2: 8,000 units symbolised in the Mayan and Aztec mathematical system (Smith and LeVeque)

Then again, even though they interpret the mathematics area of knowledge differently, the objective value of 8,000 units is still the same. For this reason, mathematics can be described as broadly universal and not tied to a particular culture. Pythagoras believed this claim, arguing that every object — irrespective of any context — in our universe has a pattern-based numerical attribute, thereby explaining how mathematical knowledge persists without any cultural involvement (Huffman). However, even linguistics can be used to describe the world around us objectively. Music is also pattern-based. As such, is his notion of the infinitely describable nature of the world through mathematics a justified belief found to be true, knowledge discovered millennia ago, or is it a conceit of culture? Since Pythagoras's research into mathematics was built on his experiences, his belief itself is arguably influenced by culture.

Furthermore, it may be true that *mathematics* exists independent of culture, but this does not mean mathematical *knowledge* is independent of culture. This is substantiated by the cultural parallel between knowledge in mathematics and the arts. For instance, just as the arts have paradigm shifts such as Realism, the maths have groundbreaking discoveries, such as imaginary numbers. It took four centuries for Girolamo Cardano's seminal invention of imaginary numbers to be accepted, developed, and adopted as common knowledge (Honner). Conceivably, it was difficult for mathematicians to work with imaginary numbers as their preexisting culture in the study of mathematics only permitted practical values. However, after Caspar Wessel was able to derive the geometry of imaginary numbers using points in a plane, more mathematicians understood and thereby accepted the significance of imaginary numbers; ergo, a paradigm shift in the culture of mathematics as mathematician's thought processes concerning imaginary numbers rapidly changed ("Caspar Wessel").

Mathematics outside proof, theory, and thought can also be influenced by culture. For instance, the application of mathematics in our lives, which is arguably just as important in generating knowledge and invoking meaning, is tied to culture heavily. In the historical development of architecture, mathematical progress in geometry was used to design structures that reflected societal and, effectively, cultural ideals and norms. For instance, the "secret" of Brunelleschi's dome in Florence (Figure 3), coined by Professor Corazzi from the University of Florence (2013), is in the underlying mathematics.

Figure 3: The mathematical symmetry of Brunelleschi's dome in Florence, Italy (Corazzi)

Brunelleschi designed the dome in 1418, using mathematical angle and circle theorems prevalent in the Renaissance, to reflect a new cultural ideal in Italy—symmetry. In fact, mathematical knowledge was significantly used during the Renaissance to reflect cultural ideals, as geometry was essential in the generation of symmetrical structures (Corazzi). Ultimately, since the expression of mathematics is bound to culture; there is evidence for paradigm shifts in mathematical theories; and mathematics can be applied to represent cultural ideals, the claim that mathematical knowledge is entirely independent of culture is refuted.

In conclusion, we now see that there is always a genuine relationship between knowledge in mathematics and the arts and culture, more so when culture is defined broadly. It is intriguing to see how these, arguably, contrasting areas of knowledge are both influenced by culture in real-world applications. Ultimately, there can be knowledge independent of culture—on the surface level. However, once that surface is uncovered, it is apparent how identity, experience, and society affect and enrich the knowledge understood and generated in our world. Through the same lens, the knowledge I generate through my learning, whether in art, mathematics, or any class for that matter, is also enriched by culture.

Works Cited

"Caspar Wessel and Complex Numbers." *Mathematics at University of Colorado Denver*, U of Colorado Denver, www.math.ucdenver.edu/ rrosterm/wessel/wessel.html. Accessed 28 Feb. 2022.

Corazzi, Roberto. "The Secret of Brunellesci's Dome and the Mathematics." *Silo*, 2013, silo.tips/download/the-secret-of-brunellesci-s-dome-and-the-mathematics. Accessed 28 Feb. 2022.

Honner, Patrick. "The (Imaginary) Numbers at the Edge of Reality." *QuantaMagazine*, 25 Oct. 2018, www.quantamagazine.org/the-imaginary-numbers-at-the-edge-of-reality-20181025/. Accessed 28 Feb. 2022.

Huffman, Carl. "Pythagoreanism." *Stanford Encyclopedia of Philosophy*, Metaphysics Research Lab, 29 Mar. 2006, plato.stanford.edu/entries/pythagoreanism/. Accessed 28 Feb. 2022.

Khoshdel, Dara Djavan. "2012 Experiments - Art and Emotion." *BBC*, 2012, www.bbc.co.uk/radio4/features/sywtbas/finalists/art/. Accessed 28 Feb. 2022.

Lee, Kitmin. *Blue Monochrome. Levy Gorvy,* www.levygorvy.com/works/yves-klein-la-revoluti-on-bleue/. Accessed 3 Mar. 2022.

Murphy, and J. Stephen. "Jamming the Machine: Yves Klein's Blue Monochrome and the End of the Avant-Garde." *eScholarship,* University of California Los Angeles, 1996, escholarship.org/conte-nt/qt3d48x20g/qt3d48x20g.pdf?t=krnn0t. Accessed 28 Feb. 2022.

Smith, David, and William LeVeque. "Numeral systems." *Britannica,* Encyclopædia Britan-nica, www.britannica.com/science/numeral/Numeral-systems. Accessed 28 Feb. 2022.

Stafford, Tom. "Do we all see the same colours?" *BBC,* 14 Feb. 2012, www.bbc.com/future/art-icle/20120209-do-we-all-see-the-same-colours. Accessed 1 Mar. 2022.

Appendix A: Politics by Carol Ann Duffy

How it makes of your face a stone
that aches to weep, of your heart a fist,
clenched or thumping, sweating blood, of your tongue
an iron latch with no door. How it makes of your right hand
a gauntlet, a glove-puppet of the left, of your laugh
a dry leaf blowing in the wind, of your desert island discs
hiss hiss hiss, makes of the words on your lips dice
that can throw no six. How it takes the breath
away, the piss, makes of your kiss a dropped pound coin,
makes of your promises latin, gibberish, feedback, static,
of your hair a wig, of your gait a plankwalk. How it says this –
politics – to your education education education; shouts this –
Politics! – to your health and wealth; how it roars, to your
conscience moral compass truth, POLITICS POLITICS POLITICS.

EXAMPLE 5

<u>Title:</u> Is ambiguity a shortcoming of language that must be eliminated, or can it also be seen as making a positive contribution to knowledge and knowing?

<u>Grade:</u> A

<u>Author:</u> Anonymous

<u>Session:</u> May 2022

Research Question: Is ambiguity a shortcoming of language that must be eliminated, or can it also be seen as making a positive contribution to knowledge and knowing?

"There is no greater impediment to the advancement of knowledge than the ambiguity of words" A quote by Thomas Reid. The Scottish philosopher believed that ambiguity hindered the advancement of knowledge and should be eliminated but his perspective is highly debatable as it can be argued that ambiguity is highly essential to the discussion of language. Before further discussion, it is necessary to know what is meant by the word "ambiguity". According to the Cambridge dictionary, ambiguity refers to the possibility that something can have more than one interpretation, the object itself is doubtful or uncertain. Through a certain perspective, ambiguity can be seen as a shortcoming of language but comparatively, it can also be seen as a positive contribution.

According to many renowned linguists, ambiguity should be considered as shortcoming of language that hinders the communication of information. They propose the question of why words should have different meanings that could possibly lead to the miscommunication of information when the purpose of language is the opposite. MIT linguistic Professor Noam Chomsky believed that ambiguity was a "design flaw" in language and that each word should have a singular meaning to avoid any sort of misunderstanding or argument in the communication of information. Languages are systems created to convey information between a speaker and a listener, it is argued that by eliminating ambiguity we remove chances of miscommunication or manipulation. For example, politicians use ambiguity in their campaigns and speeches to gain popularity amongst a larger crowd. If politicians have clear goals that they identify, they will also have a large group of people that oppose their goals and ideology. However, if they have ambiguous goals that they don't clarify to their audience, they leave it up to interpretations and will therefore be able to appeal to a larger group of people. Specifically, we can look at 1930s German elections, where Hitler campaigned around the central idea "Volksgemeinschaft" which means - people's community. Through this open-ended campaign, Hitler gained popularity by promising a return to a conservative community for the people. The German citizens justified different means to this promised end and Hitler gained popularity. While this use of ambiguity is manipulative, it can also be seen as a technique for effective use of language.

Opposingly, according to MIT cognitive science professor Ted Gibson, ambiguity makes a positive contribution to knowledge by letting us reuse the same words in a multitude of different contexts to convey different meanings. He proposed the meaning of a word comes from the context it is presented in and miscommunications can be avoided by disambiguating the word through the context. Natural languages are highly ambiguous and commonly words have more than one meaning and these word advance languages by letting them by open to interpretation and continuously changing. For example, the word "mean" can be understood in a variety of different ways depending on the context. The word "mean" can be defined to "indicate or signify something"; it can be referred to as an offensive action; it can refer to as an intention (I meant to do my homework) or it can be look at through math, as an average of a set of numbers. The ambiguity of the word could lead to a misunderstanding between a speaker and a listener when trying to convey information but if the context is used correctly, then the word's ambiguity is only beneficial and a positive contribution to the exhibition of knowledge.

In conclusion, from the discussion above it can be deduced that ambiguity is both a short coming and positive contribution depending on the language and context it is used in. A lot of significant linguist professors theorize that with the continuous change of language, ambiguity will be removed. However, the can be contradicted by all the recent theories suggesting that ambiguity advances our languages by letting words be reused in a variety of ways to communicate different meanings.

EXAMPLE 6

<u>Title:</u> "We will always learn more about human life and human personality from novels than from scientific psychology". Would you agree? Why?

<u>Grade:</u> A

<u>Author:</u> Anonymous

<u>Session:</u> May 2018

Noam Chomsky was an American theoretical linguist who revolutionized the field of linguistics by treating it as a biologically based cognitive concept. It was his mutual interest in cognitive sciences and literature that made him believe that that "*we will always learn more about human life and human personality from novels than from scientific psychology*". While it is true that one can never 'always' learn from a single way of knowing, Chomsky's claim, to a great extent, intrigues us to evaluate the effectiveness of using literature over scientific experiments in the field of Psychology. Human life, in my opinion, is the highest expression of nature; a stage of evolution where 'nature' can think about its own thoughts, qualities, feelings, and characteristics. René Descartes, on the other hand, viewed human personality as the product of the interaction of divine and primal forces.

Primarily, both ways of knowing, Literature (i.e., Novels) and Psychology, can be regarded as equally credible ways to justify claims. While Psychology involves extensive research and scientific study of the mind and behavior, writing Literary works is a similar deliberate process that takes care, planning, time, and study. As a matter of fact, sometimes novels can involve greater use of research even than a scientific study: for example, *Cold Mountain* by Charles Frazier is a novel, despite being a fictional piece of work, relies meticulously on vast amounts of research to recreate the perfect atmosphere with a fake-realistic world that makes it so powerful and popular.

Moreover, Literature and Psychology are not always adversative to each other, for instance, psychological theories and phenomena are often demonstrated in Novels. While the novels use the expression of storytelling, they present readers the same, or sometimes, even more, ways of explaining that are, to a great extent, more potent for the readers. Novels allow the readers to literally see into the reader's mind through various dramatic devices, and while the Psychology textbooks might accomplish a similar task in the form of cross-sections or diagrams of the brain, usually, the examples in Novels are more illuminating for readers and therefore, perform a better job at teaching about human life and personality. An example of this is a book from my Literature class, *A Streetcar Named Desire* by Tennessee Williams. While in this book, the development of Blanche DuBois, the protagonist of the play, is portrayed as a mentally disturbed character, when we were analyzing the play in class, we found that the psycho-analytical lens of Literature provided a more compelling understanding of Blanche's nature and personality because of her actions in the past, rather than theoretical Psychology.

Alfred Adler, argued that "*all human accomplishment is spurred by the feelings of inferiority and innate desire to triumph over other humans, especially our siblings.*" This should not sound unfamiliar as siblings competition and feelings of inferiority are frequent themes in Novels. For example, in the novel *Little Women* by Louisa May Alcott, Jo March is characterized as a tomboy who is unladylike, boyish, and improper. Jo worries that these are defects that she shall never overcome, but her "playing brother" to her sisters and acting as man of the house while her father is at war gives her a feeling of real responsibility to her family. Her desire to support them stimulates her literary ambitions and ultimately, she compensates for her "boyish" behavior by becoming the main breadwinner of the household through her writing. The question that arises now is, whose explanation is more helpful? While Adler manages to connect his theory to all human psychology, Alcott, on the contrary, presents a personal prose that is more concrete, relevant and emotionally evocative.

After all, few people have experience in the psychologist's realm of the brain, but all of us have lived life and witnessed at least parts of what the novelists are speaking about. And we respond better to what we understand and have experienced ourselves — Scarlett O'Hara in Margaret Mitchell's Gone with the Wind could never be considered lovable or likeable in real life. Even within the novel she is too "turbulent, willful" and coarse to be "really liked". However Scarlett frequently appears on lists of "most beloved" characters of all time. She is loved because her actions are so completely understandable to everyone. Everything she does make sense in the scope of her feelings and her humanity, from her selfish self-preservationist actions to her naïve teenage dreams.

However, it is the fantasy element of novels, including fairies like Tinker Belle, which often makes people dismiss novels as unimportant, when compared to psychology. I've already addressed the fact that despite being a fictional creation, novels can still convey the same ideas as psychology, but in some cases the "fantasy" or "incredible" elements of novels can actually improve and highlight the messages, as it is removed from ordinary constraints. For example, *Ender's Game and Speaker for the Dead* by Orson Scott Card take place in worlds and galaxies that we could never possibly reach. However, by reading the novels, readers can still learn about humanity. In these novels, Card teaches an important lesson about human guilt. A basic psychology textbook explains that guilt probably developed to makes us behave more compassionately to each other. This shows us what it is — Card shows us its power by creating a society that spends thousands of years reviling itself for an act of what Card terms "xenocide." In his world, the guilt is strong enough to permeate an entire culture. Some might say that such a fantasy world is too far removed from our own to legitimately such a comparison, but the power of guilt is strong in many cultures. The idea that we bear guilt for the genocide of the Jews in the 1940's is particularly powerful. Many countries, including Germany, Austria, France, Israel, Switzerland, Poland and Belgium have enforceable laws against those who would deny it happened, and "remember the Holocaust" is still a rallying cry in many political forums.

Furthermore, while novels are infinitely more useful than psychology in understanding humanity, they do have their drawbacks. Novels are very much products of their time, and are the work of only person. A novel, once written and published, cannot be changed despite agreement that such a change would improve it. Novels also can become dated as certain methods of storytelling or even situations become less relevant. Psychology is often a collaborative science, and is open to review and revision — one only has to look at the way perceptions and treatments of serious mental illness have changed to realize how beneficial such revision can be.

Perhaps, despite the risk of becoming dated or irrelevant, novels retain a power to capture imagination and attention far beyond psychology. With In Cold Blood Truman Capote revolutionized the idea of narrating the truth in his chilling novel of a seemingly random and incredibly brutal murder. I can attest to the power of Capote's narrative — I was too terrified to even finish In Cold Blood. On the other hand, a websites suggestion that a typical serial killer might have holes in their conscience, like "Swiss cheese" merely bored me, and the complex discussion of the sociopathic killer versus the psychopathic killer confused me. It was In Cold Blood that kept me awake at night, and it achieved this through the power of narrative.

Ultimately even Adler admits that each human is unique, and to apply a generalized form of psychology to humanity is impossible. Novelists take what they know about humanity, great or little, and apply it into a real world, in the way that is best perceived and understood. Therefore, narrative storytelling is one of the most powerful methods of communication, because it allows the reader to witness ideas and situations in an environment that could possibly, maybe, someday, happen to them. Lastly, based on the aforementioned claims, it can be concluded that while Scientific Psychology is undoubtedly great in learning the theoretical knowledge about human life and personality, Novels actually take an uncommon approach in the way that they teach a more applicative version of the same.

EXAMPLE 7

<u>Title:</u> "Too much of our knowledge revolves around ourselves, as if we are the most important thing in the universe"(adapted from Carlo Rovelli)."How might this be problematic?

<u>Grade:</u> A

<u>Author:</u> Anonymous

<u>Session:</u> May 2020

"Too much of our knowledge revolves around ourselves, as if we are the most important thing in the universe" (adapted from Carlo Rovelli)." How might this be problematic?

World count: 1589

Society often holds those who are selfless in high regard. But as we often view and experience the world through our own perspective, it can be difficult to distinguish who and what is really selfless. The prescribed title to me, is an interesting concept that is highly relevant to our current society. This is because knowledge that currently exists is generally focused on ourselves, as viewing the world through our own perspective may limit our awareness for our surroundings. Therefore, I believe that "too much" knowledge revolving around ourselves will be problematic. This will be discussed through the Arts and the Human Sciences as I believe that personal input is integral in the development of knowledge in these AOKs. Subjective terms such as knowledge that "revolves around ourselves" is defined as knowledge that is self-centred and focused on the individual. Furthermore, "problematic" is defined to be a cause of limitations for knowledge acquisition.

The scope of Human Sciences often aims to investigate a knower's behaviours in the natural world. However, "too much" personal knowledge might be problematic as it can negatively influence a knower's behaviours in the natural world. For example, as a part of my Economics course, I am learning about the effectiveness of foreign aid in developing countries. A common viewpoint towards aid is that it is effective as it allows for an increase in economic development. However, many economists such as Angus Deaton disagree with this and argue that aid is not effective (Swanson, 2015). Deaton's opinion towards aid has stemmed from an overreliance in his personal knowledge of studying links between aid and corruption. Consequently, allowing for him to formulate his own personal process to reason with knowledge within developmental economics. Contrary to Deaton's aid argument, there have been situations where aid has been effective such as through micro-credit lending schemes, (Swanson, 2015). Hence, Deaton relying on his personal reason to distinguish that aid is ineffective might be problematic as it could potentially limit the scope of knowledge in developmental economics through discrediting previous successful aid initiatives. Therefore, "too much" personal knowledge that revolves around ourselves might be problematic in the Human Sciences as it limits the depth of knowledge that is able to be acquired. This could have further negative ramifications where the scope of knowledge that is available in this AOK could be limited by our self-centered knowledge.

Contrastingly, the influence of personal knowledge in artistic creation can allow for knowledge in the Arts to influence an artist's audience to possess a new outlook towards a specific style of art, and hence perform a social function. One example of this is through Lily Yeh, an artist who has curated various artworks that were inspired by the personal experiences and stories of various refugees (Williams, 2020). Yeh's choice to represent refugees' stories is based on her own personal emotions towards the subject matter. While Yeh's artwork is focused on her connection to the stories of refugees, it is still able to create significant meaning for the audience even though they also possess their own personal knowledge. Besides, our self-centred knowledge can influence the way that we interpret an art piece. This allows for Lily Yeh to perform a social function through her artworks as the audience can share the experience of gaining an understanding from her artwork and adopt a more open-minded perspective of the world. Hence, she is shaping her audience's understanding of the world. In the Arts, the interpretation of an art piece by an audience is subjected to the knowledge which revolves around themselves. Art is loosely defined and often has a myriad of interpretations. Investing too much personal knowledge in the Arts can provide material and allow for the audience to form their own emotional connection to an art piece. Hence, allowing for the arts to perform a social function by shaping the audience's view of the world through being subjected to new knowledge in an art piece.

My personal stance has not changed after analysing the scope of knowledge in the Arts and Human Sciences because there is still a problematic element of bias which can be attributed to knowledge revolving around ourselves.

On the contrary, possessing "too much" personal knowledge might be problematic as it can restrict the acquisition of knowledge in the Arts. The acquisition of knowledge within the Arts can result from personal biases which is linked to our personal knowledge. I always find that my music taste is different to my friends and family. Perhaps, self-centred knowledge can also influence how we appreciate and draw connections to music. Upon further research, I found an article which suggests that there is a link between music and self-identity (Siemann, 2017). This viewpoint is compelling as it considers that emotions may influence our ability to connect with an artist's creativity and imagination. As a result, our personal emotions can determine whether we can draw knowledge from a piece of music and how we understand the piece of art. Consequently, "too much" personal knowledge could hinder our ability to acquire an open-minded view towards knowledge in the Arts as it can often be difficult to separate knowledge from personal identity. This might be problematic as it can result in disagreements about the value of art in society. But it also allows for there to be a wide-range of genres in music which cater to the different tastes and experiences of each individual, allowing for the arts to be enjoyed by more people in society. As a result, there are instances where too much knowledge revolving around ourselves can negatively influence the appreciation we hold for knowledge in the arts through our ability to emotionally connect to it. However, the ability for there to be individual, self-centred knowledge has allowed for there to be a large range of art which can appeal to a wider audience through an emotional connection.

Additionally, my personal stance has not changed but I need to also consider whether the influence of personal knowledge is always problematic in every situation.

Despite personal knowledge restricting knowledge acquisition in the Arts, in the Human Sciences, self-centered knowledge may not be problematic as the development of personal knowledge can facilitate the achievement of an understanding of human behavior. Knowledge in the Human Sciences can allow for an achievement of an understanding of self, as a conscious individual which often possesses their own personal knowledge. For instance, in an article written by Forbes (2020) there was an exploration of the benefits of humans behaving to be self-serving in business. The article discusses how being "selfish" can be motivating in a business as it can allow for there to be increased chances of success and that prioritizing oneself can allow for motivation to focus on weaknesses in a business which can allow for the growth of a company (Burns, 2020). Typically, these behaviors would be seen as negative as they are only beneficial to an individual. However, this may not be problematic as too much self-centered knowledge can still facilitate human motivation which can allow for the knower to acquire knowledge that may increase their motivation. This can allow for the growth of knowledge in an individual which can be beneficial to both the individual and society. Hence, the possession of self-centered knowledge might not always be problematic in the Human Sciences as it can allow for an understanding of an individual's behavior and the acquisition of knowledge which is beneficial to an individual and their personal motivations. In general, this does not completely support my initial stance as it demonstrates that obtaining more self-centered knowledge can facilitate the further acquisition of knowledge in the Human Sciences. I think that my conclusion towards my personal stance needs to recognise that personal knowledge still plays an essential role in knowledge acquisition despite potentially being problematic.

Whilst it is important to understand that personal focused knowledge could potentially have a problematic influence, it is important to note that it will never always be problematic that "too much knowledge revolves around ourselves." This is largely due to the essay exploring perspectives where self-centered knowledge has been problematic and where it has not been problematic through claims and counterclaims. However, these claims and counterclaims were explored through my own personal parameters for the prescribed title and hence, another person's understanding of the prescribed title may result in a different conclusion.

Additionally, this can be explored in many different perspectives such as through other AOKs such as mathematics, where too much self-centered knowledge may not be problematic as knowledge in mathematics is reliant on logic and reason. For instance, a mathematician, Po-Shen Loh, developed a new formula for the quadratic formula through relying upon his personal knowledge which revolved around his interest in mathematics. This allowed for him to change the scope of understanding surrounding the quadratic formula as many individuals may find this formula *"easier to understand,"* (Loh, 2019) compared to the standard formula. Hence, I believe that the degree of problems that may arise with too much self-centered knowledge is dependent on the AOK and the actual scenario.

My initial stance has slightly changed as there are many examples where it is not problematic that too much of our knowledge revolves around ourselves as it can assist in knowledge acquisition and contribute to our understanding of self. Despite this, there are still scenarios where too much personal knowledge can be problematic. Hence, I now believe that although having too much self-centered knowledge might be problematic, its existence is still crucial for the process of knowledge acquisition and allows for us to communicate our knowledge to other people.

World count: 1589

114

Reference List

Burns, S. (2020, March 12). *6 Ways Being Selfish Can Make You Successful*. Retrieved from
    Forbes:
    https://www.forbes.com/sites/stephanieburns/2020/03/12/6-ways-being-selfish-can-m
    ake-you-successful/#3390618e5538

Loh, P.-S. (2019). *A Different Way to Solve Quadratic Equations*. Retrieved from Po-Shen
    Loh: https://www.poshenloh.com/quadratic/

Siemann, I. (2017, March 21). *The impact of music on identity*. Retrieved from The McGill
    Tribune:
    https://www.mcgilltribune.com/sci-tech/the-impact-of-music-on-identity-032117/

Swanson, A. (2015, October 23). *Does foreign aid always help the poor?* Retrieved from
    World Economic Forum :
    https://www.weforum.org/agenda/2015/10/does-foreign-aid-always-help-the-poor/

Williams, J. (2020, March 11). *Visualizing the Refugee Experience*. Retrieved from The New
    York Times:
    https://www.nytimes.com/2020/03/11/arts/visualizing-refugee-experience.html

EXAMPLE 8

<u>Title:</u> "The quality of knowledge is best measured by how many people accept it." Discuss this claim with reference to two areas of knowledge.

<u>Grade:</u> A

<u>Author:</u> Anonymous

<u>Session:</u> May 2021

1. **"The quality of knowledge is best measured by how many people accept it." Discuss this claim with reference to two areas of knowledge.**

To reword this prompt, I would say, the value of knowledge is best determined by its popularity and acceptance. It is claiming the quality of knowledge increases in accreditation as the quantity of believers increase. But in dissecting this prescribed title, its necessary to establish definitions of quality, knowledge, and best, so we can explore this claim thoroughly. To me, quality is synonymous to worth or value. Knowledge, while defined as "the sum of what is known; the body of truth, info, and principles acquired by humankind," is basically information or beliefs (Merriam Webster). Best is the most subjective word because even its definition requires personal judgement, "most productive of good : offering or producing the greatest advantage, utility, or satisfaction"(Merriam Webster).

To properly dive into my beliefs of this claim, I must examine group knowledge versus personal knowledge, looking at the value of both. In broader terms, I disagree with the claim "The quality of knowledge is best measured by how many people accept it" because the value placed on knowledge is dependent on the personal beliefs of the individual rather than a societal norm. Additionally, there are many holes in using the amount of believers as a measuring stick for knowledge. I will explore this claim in relation to Religious Knowledge Systems because it is usually associated with Faith and Intuition. In these Religious systems, there is a common theme of "group doctrines" and this tendency to value group knowledge will be an interesting perspective to examine. Because the Natural Sciences rely more on Reason and Sense Perception, I chose to explore this Area of Knowledge to contrast the previous perspective.

Religious Knowledge Systems have been in existence for all of recorded history, and therefore, they play a crucial role in the development of cultures. Countless peoples have looked to Religion to determine the organization of their civilization, even relying on it for moral decisions. This being said, the range of Religions mean there are numerous knowledge systems based around these religions. And with thousands of religions, there are various types and sub-types of faiths, such as Christianity and within that Catholicism. The string that ties all of these belief systems together is composed of group doctrines. A doctrine is defined by Merriam Webster as "a principle or position or the body of principles in a branch of knowledge or system of belief." Basically, each religion relies on the participants of said religion to fully believe in the doctrine associated with said religion. For example, Jewish people are able to bond over their shared belief in Judaism furthering the quality of that doctrine.

With this being said, is one religious knowledge system higher quality because it has more followers than another smaller-scale religious system? I say no. The quality cannot be judged based on how many people accept it because there are many confounding factors that influence one's acceptance of such system, such as upbringing, location, and laws. For example, my friend, Tony, grew up only ever knowing Christianity, and so he become a Christian. Christianity gained another person that accepts their knowledge system. Does that mean Christianity is better quality than, say, Judaism, because it has more followers? Or does that mean because Christianity is more popularly known and practiced, it is more easily accessible? I believe quality does not directly correspond to quantity of believers, especially in reference to Religious Knowledge Systems.

However, accepting knowledge within religion can become tricky. Generally, religious knowledge systems prefer followers to adhere to their doctrine strictly or at least avoid questioning or doubting it. In this sense, the quality of knowledge could be determined by the amount of those accepting of it. Properly developed Religious Knowledge Systems would have more followers than a poorly established system because it would work for more people. To put this in context, a new religious cult based around a niche branch of scientology may not have strong organization and therefore has less followers. In this hypothetical example, people have abandoned this cult because its disorganized and the different interpretations of the doctrine don't match the initial values stated by the cult founder. We could measure the quality of this Religious Knowledge System by how many people accept it because there's a clear connection between the quality of the knowledge and the dissatisfaction of the followers.

Exploring another Area of Knowledge, it's important to note how this prescribed title applies to the Natural Sciences. This area of knowledge focuses on reasoning and sense perception, and the large logic component of this area makes it reliable. The Natural Sciences deal with making observations about the physical world, rather than the human sciences. The world of science revolves around labs, experiments, and research. These all sound extremely soundproof because they are based in reason and have many practical applications, but if we dive deeper into this world, it's clear that not all scientific knowledge is valued the same.

Most scientists look at publishing research as the crowning glory of their jobs because they can share their work with the world. While this happens for quite a lot of scientists, not all research ends up being published. Scientific journals avoid publishing research that supports an unpopular conclusion because it could be a source of potential conflict within the science world. As a scientist working for the Food and Drug Administration, I would want my findings to support the company's wishes because this could secure my job. If I found that vape pens are harmful to the lungs due to the inhalation of nicotine vapor, but the FDA has been sponsored by Juul, a vape company, then my research would not be seen as valuable to my company. This hypothetical research could harm the public's view of vape pens making them less likely to purchase them from the Juul company. If Juul loses business, then the FDA loses a sponsor.

Thinking this concept through, our knowledge about the natural sciences is very much skewed because we only know the published research. Because some research isn't published because it doesn't have a strong correlation or it has negative results, the Natural Sciences provide a swift opportunity to apply the prescribed title. The quality of knowledge, in this case: scientific knowledge, cannot be measured simply by the number of people that accept it. The quality of scientific knowledge lays within the operating methods used by the scientists during the experiment and the authenticity of results. Saying this, quality is irrelevant to a study being published or not. Research is often published based on the usefulness of the results which in itself raises a question of ethics: In what ways is it unethical for a scientist to not publish their research solely because their results do not match their intended or desired results? The Scientist is a crucial perspective to examine since it encompasses both ethics and the natural sciences, requiring intuition and emotion.

To place this into an example, I created a study design for my Sports, Exercise, and Health Science internal assessment. This asked participants to run around different formations of cones, but they were also asked a series of questions used to determine their sleeping pattern. The overall goal of my experiment was to find the relationship between sleep deprivation and physical reflexes, but the results never showed a clear cut relationship. I followed the principles of study design (having a control group, double-blinding, and using correct tools, etc), but the results were inconclusive. The quality of the knowledge, or the results I found from this experiment, is not less than another study with either an extreme negative or positive correlation. If each experiment is carried out ethically and properly, the quality of the knowledge has no connection to the actual results. Bringing this back to the prescribed title, the amount of people that accept a certain piece of knowledge is mostly dependent on their accessibility to that knowledge, so it is unfair to claim that the quality of knowledge somehow decreases if less people accept it. A study seen by ten people isn't any less valid than a study seen by a thousand people. They are simply on different scales, but there quality has not decreased.

However, it is possible that the amount of supporters of a piece of scientific knowledge is positively related to the quality of that knowledge. The more people that examine research, the more people there are to poke holes in it, so if a certain study has thousands of supporters, it can be said that there is probably few or no mistakes within that study because it's survived lots of scrutiny. Although previously I completely disagreed with the statement used in the prompt, within Natural Sciences, the quality of the knowledge can occasionally be attributed to the amount of people that accept said knowledge.

In general, I have observed the variety of situations where the quality of knowledge is indirectly connected to the amount of supporters, such as in accepting published research or diving into religion. There are cases where it is best to assess quality based on popularity, but because these cases are particular, it's best to separate number of acceptors from the quality of that piece of knowledge. It's important to recognize this because by avoiding unfair judgements of knowledge, we are opening ourselves up to absorb more knowledge. It's crucial to examine each situation within its own context to assess the role the supporters play in validating the knowledge, but by being more open to knowledge, we are able to create our own conclusions rather than rely on generalizations.

Word Count: 1,599

Bibliography

"Best." *Merriam-Webster*, Merriam-Webster, www.merriam-webster.com/dictionary/best.

"Knowledge." *Merriam-Webster*, Merriam-Webster, www.merriam-webster.com/dictionary/knowledge.

EXAMPLE 9

<u>Title:</u> "If a disagreement about knowledge claims needs to be resolved, then it is essential to give equal attention to both sides". Under what circumstances is this good advice?

<u>Grade:</u> A

<u>Author:</u> Anonymous

<u>Session:</u> November 2020

In the Natural and Human Sciences, scientists' differing perspectives can lead to disagreements regarding how to best resolve disagreements about knowledge claims. Applying the quotation to this context, the proposition that disagreement "needs to be resolved" implies that scientists favour consensus over controversy. However, arriving at complete agreement is often complicated, given these differing views. Additionally, the word "essential" entails that giving attention to "both sides" is imperative. "Both sides" suggests a binary argument, whereas in both sciences there tend to be multiple perspectives on knowledge claims. Even so, how do we determine the right balance of attention that is provided to each of these sides? While disagreements can hinder progress by creating uncertainty during the initial stages of knowledge production, they can aid the pursuit of knowledge by offering multiple perspectives on a knowledge claim, providing knowers with a more comprehensive understanding of the truth.

When proposing hypotheses in the natural sciences, it might be more essential for scientists to establish their knowledge claims through inductive reasoning first, focusing on one side. This provides the hypothesis with credibility before any efforts are made to falsify it, as excessive disagreement in the early stages of knowledge production stalls scientific progress. When proposing the idea of using Bangladesh's potato surplus in a biofuel industry for my Extended Essay (EE) (combining Chemistry and Economics), I was convinced that this measure could have a significant impact on the country's development. However, while researching, I encountered numerous arguments for and against biofuels. For example, while emissions were far lower than those of fossil fuels, biofuels were far less energy efficient. I also found other renewable sources that performed far better in both emissions and efficiency. However, I decided to initially focus on sources that supported my proposed solution to the energy crisis in Bangladesh, giving less attention to counterarguments. While this approach could be argued to have confirmation bias, initially focusing on the "for" side allowed me to construct a coherent argument to start with. So in the initial stages of knowledge generation, it is better advice to focus attention on one side.

The limitation of establishing hypotheses by focusing only on compatible evidence, however, is that scientists tend to be pervaded towards reinforcing their knowledge claim rather than the scientific knowledge itself. Prior to my EE, I had a preconceived notion that renewable sources were invariably better than fossil fuels overall. As a result, I initially only pursued information that supported my claim, overlooking contradictory evidence. However, giving equal attention to counterarguments in my evaluation allowed me to gain a more complex understanding of the situation. I found that biofuels, in fact, produce similar emissions, and as explained earlier, they are far less efficient. With crop-based biofuels, there are issues such as food versus fuel and uncertainty regarding poor weather, amongst others. While initially focusing on arguments for biofuels allowed me to establish biofuels' potential in Bangladesh, exploring alternative views offered insight into potential pitfalls, and clarified misconceptions regarding sustainability. Falsifying the proposed hypothesis allows a scientist to explore inconsistencies, developing a more rounded understanding of the claim in contention. Therefore, once the potential of a hypothesis is justified by supporting evidence, it is advisable to shift attention to the process of falsification.

An alternative view on the prescribed title is that once hypotheses are established, scientists rely on disagreement within the scientific community to test their hypothesis. Differences in data interpretation can mean that equally qualified scientists can disagree. When this occurs, it may be essential to consider various arguments equally, given the scientists' level of experience. A recent article discusses the reliability of genomic footprinting in classifying a hominid species found in Indonesia (Nature Methods, 2016). One group of scientists promoted the capabilities of such technology in determining relationships between DNA structures and a species' characteristics. Employing parallel sequencing technology, the group produced data that helped obtain information on transcription factor binding: a crucial step in the classification of organisms. A second group raised issues regarding the use of genomic footprinting, arguing that such analysis would be inadequate. Instead, they studied nuclear receptors to understand the effects of chromatin on gene expression. Although the perspectives on the reliability of genomic footprinting are contradictory, it is essential to give equal attention to both approaches, as a fair review of the argument could generate new evidence, and allow scientists to develop modified methodologies. Using one group's sequencing techniques in conjunction with the second group's studies on receptors may further elucidate the preferences of certain transcription factors. Furthermore, allowing scientists to impartially compare their opinions reduces confirmation bias, as they are made to assess different situations from a new perspective, strengthening their understanding of their claims. Under these circumstances, giving equal attention to alternative approaches is essential, as it facilitates the production of well-rounded knowledge.

Nevertheless, when scientists have multiple approaches to resolving claims, how should one balance attention between their methodologies? In economics, under what circumstances is it acceptable to give more attention to one model over another? Classical and Keynesian economists disagree on government intervention in the market, with Keynesian theory suggesting that government expenditure is necessary to promote aggregate demand after a certain point in time (Blink & Dorton, 2011). My economics IA involved writing a commentary on the potential impacts of interest rate cuts in Australia. The IA requires students to choose one approach, and my teacher promoted the Classical approach, arguing for its simplicity. Focusing on one approach at that stage was acceptable, as it served the purpose of straightforwardly developing my basic economic knowledge. Nonetheless, doing so only offers a one-sided understanding of how the final result was obtained, which might be sufficient for a high-school student to grasp basic economic phenomena, but it doesn't encourage reflection upon the inevitable interaction of the various factors affecting the economy. In the context of my high-school learning, however, it is less necessary to reach resolution. While equally considering disagreements would be beneficial in strengthening the knower's understanding, it is acceptable to focus on one side for convenience.

However, as real-world economies are influenced by a multitude of factors, giving equal attention to different views is crucial, given the consequential nature of economic policy. This scenario also raises a potential issue with the prescribed title - isn't it possible that there are more than two sides to arguments? If so, the vigorous back-and-forth of disagreements regarding various economic factors facilitates valuable discussion, allowing policymakers to assess economic phenomena with greater reliability. In deciding whether to intervene in the market, it would be beneficial for the Australian government to offer equal attention to not only Classical and Keynesian perspectives, but also to factors such as foreign relations. While Governor Philip Lowe suggested further interest rate cuts, John Frydenberg, treasurer to Prime Minister Scott Morrison, argued that non-interventionist policies would sufficiently promote growth in the Australian economy (Karp, 2019). Giving unbiased attention to these perspectives, and also other possible viewpoints would be instrumental in allowing the Australian government to make a well-informed decision. Therefore, given the magnitude of economic decisions, it is better advice to assess contrasting economic responses fairly, as governments can then adjust their stances on market intervention, and reliably predict the impacts of their policies on different stakeholders.

When resolving interdisciplinary knowledge claims, however, giving equal attention to disagreements can hinder resolution, as scientists from different fields might have different reasons for their perspectives, which cannot necessarily be weighed up against each other because they involve different criteria. During my EE research, I studied economists and chemists with contradictory arguments regarding the effectiveness of a potato-biofuel industry. Numerous chemists argue for biofuels improving environmental sustainability through smaller emissions, whereas many businesses wish to avoid biofuels due to their low efficiency, which reduces profitability. There were several arguments for and against biofuels, like so. While exploring these arguments developed a strong understanding of the capabilities of potato-biofuels, the lack of certainty created by giving equal attention to various standpoints made me skeptical about my conclusion, as different sides undermined each other. My interdisciplinary study on this topic allowed me to realise that individuals view claims differently based on which factors they prioritize. When concluding, I suggested that it would be advisable to start with small-scale trials, giving more focus towards confirming that biofuels have a positive impact, before equally considering counterarguments. Doing this not only prevents the country from dwelling on disagreements and stalling scientific progress, but also provides a multifaceted understanding of the various possibilities. Judging the evidence in the form of the final outcome, rather than wastefully paying equal attention to disagreements in the methodology is more practical. Hence, with interdisciplinary claims, it appears to be better advice to initially focus attention to one side, before shifting attention to counterarguments between disciplines.

Overall, the level of attention given to disagreements about a knowledge claim can have differing outcomes. Illustrated by the example of determining the feasibility of biofuels, giving equal attention to conflicting sides can be detrimental, resulting in the loss of confidence in new knowledge. Instead, focusing on a one-sided argument in the initial stages of knowledge production is more appropriate. However, in both natural and human sciences, giving attention to multiple sides in the latter stages forms more robust knowledge. Taking economic decisions after an equal consideration of multiple perspectives ensures more desirable outcomes for the population. In the natural sciences, giving equal attention to alternative perspectives and anomalous evidence facilitates greater understanding of new knowledge. From critically evaluating claims made in an EE to exploring multiple standpoints while setting government policy, giving equal attention to more than one perspective opens the doors to more substantial knowledge claims.

Bibliography

Blink, J., & Dorton, I. (2011). *Economics Course Companion.* Oxford: Oxford University Press.

Karp, P. (2019, October 1). *Reserve Bank cuts interest rates to historic low of 0.75% to boost weak economy.* Retrieved May 29, 2020, from The Guardian: https://www.theguardian.com/australia-news/2019/oct/01/reserve-bank-cuts-interest-rates-to-historic-low-of-075-to-boost-flagging-economy

Nature Methods. (2016, February 25). *The power of disagreement.* Retrieved April 26, 2020, from Nature: https://www.nature.com/articles/nmeth.3798

EXAMPLE 10

<u>Title:</u> "1. Can there be knowledge that is independent of culture? Discuss with reference to mathematics and one other area of knowledge.

<u>Grade:</u> A

<u>Author:</u> Anonymous

<u>Session:</u> November 2021

Knowledge comes from humans. Humans who cannot help themselves but to be influenced by culture when creating new knowledge. And no culture affects this human production of knowledge more than the culture held within the areas of knowledge themselves. This culture, manifested through accepted interpretations, enforces standards for the scope and the appropriate methods and tools within an area of knowledge. Humans, whether adhering to or rejecting these beliefs, create knowledge that cannot exist without being shaped by culture. Thus to answer the question of "Can there be knowledge that is independent of culture?", I believe that knowledge is always dependent on culture, as the set of beliefs within each area of knowledge dictates what new ideas are considered to be appropriate and true in math and natural sciences.

First, knowledge is affected by culture as culture guides what each area of knowledge considers as their scope. In mathematics, it was common for new knowledge to be deemed inappropriate as it did not fit what mathematicians commonly thought of as the role of math — it went against an established culture. For example, when analyzing the del Ferro-Tartaglia-Cardano formula for cubic equations, Rafael Bombelli stumbled into the problem of dealing with negative numbers under square roots, which had no known solution at the time (Vohra). Thus, Bombelli introduced the imaginary number i, equal to the square root of -1. This concept solved the problem of the formula, allowing negative square roots to cancel out, yet was rejected and even mocked by the rest of the mathematical community. This was due to the fact that 16th century culture within maths saw the area of knowledge as a representation of concrete real world objects. Furthermore, the scope of mathematics was thought to be based solely on real geometry, and if a square had a negative area, then the side length did not make sense. Such an "imaginary" number could not exist in real life, and thus this new idea was not deemed proper knowledge. However, it is evident that imaginary numbers are deemed very appropriate and true knowledge today, even being accepted to describe reality in the famous Schrodinger wave equation. This corresponds to a direct shift in mathematical culture, as the area of knowledge no longer was seen as a direct representation of real-world numbers and geometry, but rather a more abstract area of knowledge that can be periodically applied to reality.

Similarly in natural sciences, pioneers in quantum mechanics such as Planck and Einstein, found concepts which went against the perceived scope of physics. They discovered concepts of quantization of energy and relativity which defied the laws of Newtonian physics that had stood for over 2 centuries (Brahambhatt). Their work showed that physics could not be explained through a set of central formulas and equations at our current capabilities, but rather an amalgamation of many seemingly unrelated models which work for different areas of physics. Newtonian physics was a great estimate for everyday situations of energy and size, but modern physics was needed to describe the world at extreme conditions such as relativity for high speeds, and Planck's constant at very small sizes. This challenged the existing cultural view held by other prominent figures within natural sciences, and was rejected as false knowledge. It took considerable time for these theories to become accepted, and since, the shift in scope has led to much improved knowledge of subatomic particles and better models of the universe through quantum mechanics. This example further shows how often this relationship between culture and knowledge may be even bidirectional, with new knowledge pulling paradigm shifts in scope, and cultural shifts spurring new knowledge.

Some may argue that objectivity is always the main focus in mathematics and natural science, and that it is simply technology and intelligence which limits what knowledge is considered true. I think that at the same time, often what is objective is not clearly defined, and thus it is largely the culture followed by mathematicians and physicists that dictates what we consider as appropriate new knowledge. The two described cases mirror many similar paradigm shifts in math, science, and other more subjective areas of knowledge in art and suggest that often the culture within an area of knowledge may limit our ability to successfully judge new knowledge. As well, cultural influence on concepts such as the imaginary number question if we can ever achieve true objectivity, even in mathematics and natural sciences. It can be argued that the culture in which we regulate knowledge may hamper the progression of new true knowledge due to the bias it creates within people. Perhaps it is human nature to reciprocate the culture around us in the knowledge we produce, and this may continue for the rest of time.

Second, knowledge is affected by culture when there are multiple competing theories, and the values regarded as most important within an area of knowledge dictates which theory is chosen. The method in which knowledge is created in natural sciences is largely through observation and hypothesis. When there exist multiple possible interpretations for the same observations, the consensus of high-standing scientists is regarded as judgement, which is culture in itself. Moreover, in natural sciences, commonly the deciding factor is which competing theory aligns the best with the principal ideals the culture prefers. A prime example of this is Occam's razor, a principle that has been followed and cited for centuries, which states that the simplest theory, or the theory with the fewest assumptions, is always preferred (*New World Encyclopedia*). For instance, the Ptolemaic model of a geocentric solar system had become overloaded with the addition of epicycles for each planet to explain their apparent retrograde motion when observed from earth. In 1543, the published Copernican model removed the need for these assumptions by introducing a model where all planets simply orbit the sun in an elliptic fashion. The simplicity of the heliocentric model greatly helped to convince the science community of its verity by Occam's razor, and provided a large advantage in its battle against the former misguided theory.

In mathematics, two theories still exist today as a tool for calculus — Newton notation and Leibniz notation. Importantly, almost all textbooks and mathematicians claim that Leibniz notation is preferred over Newton's notation, and I believe this is also due to the culture within mathematics. Firstly, this follows the culture of valuing consistency and rigorousness. Leibniz notation is clearly more consistent throughout all of calculus, especially when used for integrals and operations outside single variable derivatives. As well, it more rigorously describes the units of calculation and arguably shows the steps of calculus in a more clear manner. Secondly, following mathematical tradition, it can be argued that the choice of notation honors the feud between Lebiniz and Newton for the invention of calculus, where Newton claims to have invented it prior, but Leibniz published his ideas first. Despite both notations adequately describing basic concepts in calculus, the values which mathematical culture holds pushes Leibniz notation forward.

A counterclaim may be that the described culture of values within mathematics and natural sciences is actually the nature of the area of knowledge itself and by following these values, it is not culture but simply objectively staying as true to the area of knowledge as possible. Decisions between theories in any area of knowledge is inevitable, and valuing simplicity in science and consistency in mathematics is the only possible choice, not a product of culture. This can be backed up with how commonly this culture points us towards knowledge that is more true to reality, such as the case of the Copernican model. I believe that while this could be true, I think it is equally likely that a slight change to history or what a famous mathematician or philosopher claimed to be important would lead to drastic shifts in our knowledge and what we consider truth, as people in the pursuit of objectivity are inevitably affected by culture before them. Once again, this influence on how we create knowledge calls into question if our culture traps us in a box of knowledge we deem acceptable. Could it be that too much of a focus on ideals such as simplicity and symmetry lead us down an incorrect path which we are blind to by culture? In natural science for example, there are many concerns over new scientists trying only to look for a theory of the universe that is "super-symmetric" that may very well not exist. As a result, I believe the cultural influence on usually objective methods of creating knowledge in math and natural sciences lends a convincing argument to how knowledge in all areas are irreversibly shaped by culture.

In conclusion, all knowledge that is created by humans cannot be independent of culture. New knowledge is dependent on how the culture inside areas of knowledge views their scope as in the case of imaginary numbers and the revolution of quantum mechanics, and the methods and tools in which we create knowledge is affected by culture as in the case of the theory of oxygen and choosing between Leibniz vs Newton notation. I believe that culture's prevalence in objective areas of math and natural sciences clearly demonstrates how interconnected knowledge and culture are, for all areas of knowledge. This then calls into question to what extent our knowledge is limited by the cultures that have been built within these areas of knowledge. It may be something harmful that we should work to eliminate, or it may be a permanent characteristic of the human spirit, a welcome reminder of our imperfection as we continue our search for knowledge.

Works Cited

Brahambhatt, Rupendra. "Quantum Theory: A Scientific Revolution That Changed Physics Forever."

    Interesting Engineering, 24 June 2021,

    https://interestingengineering.com/quantum-theory-a-scientific-revolution-that-changed-physic

    s-forever. Accessed 7 Nov. 2021.

"Ockham's Razor." *New World Encyclopedia*,

    https://www.newworldencyclopedia.org/entry/Ockham%27s_razor.

Vohra, Arya. "A Mathematical History: 'Imaginary' Numbers. Part 1: What's so Imaginary?" *Medium*, 15

    Aug. 2019,

    https://medium.com/maths-dover/a-mathematical-history-imaginary-numbers-part-1-whats-so-

    imaginary-b0c0296b0fcf. Accessed 7 Nov. 2021.

Milton Keynes UK
Ingram Content Group UK Ltd.
UKHW050721090224
437484UK00007BA/64

9 781739 185107